I'M
LISTENING, LORD,
KEEP TALKING

I'm LISTENING, LORD, KEEP TALKING

Robert J. Baker

HERALD PRESS
Scottdale, Pennsylvania
Kitchener, Ontario
1981

Library of Congress Cataloging in Publication Data

Baker, Robert J., 1920-
    I'm listening, Lord, keep talking.

    1. Meditations. 2. Baker, Robert J., 1920-
I. Title.
BV4832.2.B28   242   81-4278
ISBN 0-8361-1953-3 (pbk.)   AACR2

I'M LISTENING, LORD, KEEP TALKING
Copyright © 1981 by Herald Press, Scottdale, Pa. 15683
    Published simultaneously in Canada by Herald Press,
    Kitchener, Ont. N2G 4M5
Library of Congress Catalog Card Number: 81-4278
International Standard Book Number: 0-8361-1953-3
Printed in the United States of America
Design: Alice B. Shetler/Cover art: James Converse

81 82 83 84 85 86 10 9 8 7 6 5 4 3 2 1

To several of my spiritual fathers
who taught me as a boy the value of prayer,
Claude W. Leininger and Vernon E. Reiff.

To my good wife, Anna Mae,
who typed this manuscript.

To God,
who has patiently listened to my prayers
and talked to me with both love and sternness,
both of which I needed.

CONTENTS

AUTHOR'S PREFACE

His name was *Claude Leininger,* and he was my first Sunday school superintendent. I was a young Christian of twelve; Claude was one of my spiritual fathers. Often on a Sunday morning or evening he would corner me at the rear of our small mission church, block my exit with his beyond six-foot frame, seize my hand in his, and ask, "Well, Robert, how are you getting along in your Christian life?"

The question was a piercer, a shaker. No matter how often he asked it, no matter how much I anticipated it, I always seemed pinned against the wall by Claude as he put me on the spot asking for a spiritual weather report as of that moment, not one six weeks old.

As I stuttered out my present feelings, sometimes good, sometimes bad, Claude listened attentively, but his advice was already framed. He gave it to me as soon as my report was given. "Well, Robert, just keep on reading your Bible and praying."

It was the best advice I ever received.

At present I read the Bible through twice each year, I write a Sunday school column that appears 52 times per year, and I teach a Sunday school class. Both of the latter necessitate additional Bible study.

And I pray.

But I have been fascinated recently by an aspect of prayer with which I was acquainted only vaguely in the days of Claude Leininger.

Prayer was pretty much a one-way street in those days. Daily, usually at a set time, I unloaded on God my needs, petitions, adoration, confession, thanksgiving, supplication.

On Wednesday evening at the church prayer meeting we really zeroed in on God, often talking to Him for half an hour at a stretch. We pounded the gates of heaven with our words, words that usually spelled out our requests. It was prayer meeting, and we lived up to its name. We prayed. We were half right.

I am not ridiculing. I bless my spiritual fathers, the Mennonite Church which accepted me, loved me, educated me, forgave me, used me. Maybe today, in this book, I speak of an aspect of prayer that is familiar and practiced by many. But for me it is new. I have found that prayer is a two-way street, that God talks to me.

For several years I wrote a column for the *Gospel Herald* titled "I'm Listening, Lord, Keep Talking." From week to week I shared instances in which I believed God had spoken to me. Many of those columns are included in this book, plus a large number published for the first time.

At the beginning of each meditation in this book is a verse from God's Word that He brought to me as I sat and read and reread the incident I am sharing with you, the occasion where God talked to me. As I sat at my desk, laughing or crying, sorrowing or rejoicing because of what happened, I was also moved to write a little prayer. I invite you to write your own prayer below mine. I stress in this book how God talks with us, but we must not forget to talk with Him. So, write God a little note. He'll love it.

Often the personal experiences I relate are not complementary to me. Like myself, God is a schoolteacher. I have not always been a good pupil. So He has frequently corrected me, disciplined me. He has rapped my knuckles, sent me to the principal, even suspended me, but He has never expelled me from His school of learning.

A few times I have done right and God has been generous

in His praise. But always, whether I have listened to Him or not, He has loved me.

When we think about hearing God, having Him speak to us, we usually expect His voice to come to us through His Word (the Bible), His ministers, His created world. We may add the Holy Spirit to the list of ways in which He communicates. In an epilogue at the close of this book, I discuss how God may pick a more direct route in speaking with us.

I ardently believe that God desires to talk with us as much as we desire to talk with Him. I believe that His communication can come with bell-like clarity, can be intensified, is for real.

One thing must be quickly clarified. I am not a spiritual giant. In listening to God I came lately on the scene. Family and friends who know me best will agree without hesitation that God has plenty to discuss with me. This clay has been pretty well loused up and is far from the shape that He would desire. Perhaps we hear God in direct ratio to our needs, our weaknesses, our imperfections. I hear a lot.

I suppose to some the very suggestion of listening to God's voice, saying I hear Him speak to me, indicates I should also be listening, hearing from a counselor, or psychologist, or psychiatrist.

That may be.

My only reply would be as follows: I have found it helpful in my Christian life to sense and practice, to be involved in this two-way aspect of prayer. I care not to go back to my monologue status.

I think I need to be in dialogue with God. I've found out that I do not know all the answers, that He has a few things to say to me. Say on, Lord.

Robert J. Baker
Elkhart, Indiana

I'm
LISTENING, LORD,
KEEP TALKING

Now I want you to know, brothers, that what has happened to me [Paul] has really served to advance the gospel. As a result, it has become clear ... that I am in chains for Christ. Because of my chains, most of the brothers in the Lord have been encouraged to speak the word of God more courageously and fearlessly.

Philippians 1:12-14

1 THE WRONG SCHEDULE IS THE RIGHT ONE

When I missed my plane connection in Harrisburg, Pennsylvania, because of an error in scheduling by the travel agency, I had a few words with the Lord.

I had spent the entire weekend at a church conference, having been heavily involved in the program. I was eager to get home. My God is of the size and kind that could have prevented that error from occurring in the travel agency office. During my three-hour delay in the airport terminal building, I asked the Lord if He hadn't made some mistake. God said nothing.

In Pittsburgh I changed planes for Cleveland, sat down at

a window seat, and began reading a book from my briefcase. I was still pouting.

Soon an airline stewardess came and sat down beside me. She nodded to the small gold cross I wear in my coat lapel, then at the book I was reading, and questioned with undisguised interest, "You're a Christian, aren't you?"

I smiled through my frustration, and said, "Yes."

With eyes aglow she said, "I'm a Christian too. I really get lonesome on some of my flights to talk with other Christians. I study every passenger when he boards the plane, trying to spot some little clue that would link him with Jesus Christ. I like to sit down and share with other Christians what the Lord is doing in our lives."

The frustration balloon that I had been blowing up all morning collapsed. Her enthusiasm was in such sharp contrast with my childish self-made depression.

She asked if she might stop back later in the flight and talk with me. "Of course," I said.

While she was gone I sat there and stared out the plane window. In a few minutes we were flying through gray clouds, then burst out into glorious sunshine as we rose above them. I did a lot of thinking as we flew toward Cleveland. I did some praying, some asking of forgiveness. I told the Lord that I now understood about the missed flight. I gave Him permission to change my flight schedule anytime He chose.

Later the stewardess came back and we had a happy time of sharing concerning the goodness of our Lord.

I was four hours late in getting home, but I was right on schedule from Pittsburgh to Cleveland.

Prayer Reflection

Mine: Not once, but a hundred times, I have seen it happen. What appeared to be a mistake, a hardship, even a tragedy, turns out to be You correcting the master schedule. It's uncanny the way You juggle and dovetail things together into a perfect fitting. You're tremendous, Lord!

—Amazed

Yours: _____

_____

_____

You know with all your heart and soul that not one of the good promises the Lord your God gave you has failed. Every promise has been fulfilled; not one has failed.

Joshua 23:14

2 JUMPING ON THE PROMISES

The bumper hung loosely at the back of the VW. One could move it several inches up and down. I took it to a shop that does a variety of mechanical work, including welding. A serviceman looked underneath and said matter of factly, "Your car is too old, the frame too rusted. There is nothing solid to which I can weld your bumper. Sorry."

Disappointed, I took the car as a last resort to my Christian brother, Herm, a welding specialist. He took a hasty look underneath and said, "Sure, Bob, we can fix it."

Grabbing some strap iron and his welding tools, the sparks flew briefly but assuredly for Herm. Then emerging from under the car, he threw back his welding helmet and said, "There you are, all fixed."

With gratitude, but not quite belief, I said, "You mean the bumper will really hold now?"

I saw a flicker of irritation cross Herm's face, to be quickly replaced with a smile. "Of course, it will hold. Want me to jump on it to prove it?"

Looking at 170 pounds of solid muscle on a six-foot frame, thinking of my fragile car, knowing the bumper would never be subjected to such an up-and-down force, I quickly said, "No, Herm! It's all right!"

But I was too late. The welder leaped upon the bumper and bounced up and down several times. The VW rocked violently, but the bumper remained secure.

Now I believed Herm, really believed him, and was ashamed that I questioned him at all.

Driving the bug home I thought of the incident again and again. Herm had promised me that the bumper was fixed, but I doubted the welder, the promiser.

It was a bit like God with His Word. In that Word are thousands of promises—big ones, little ones. I read them and say that they are true, yet in my mind I may question: "God, can You really do this? Can You really cut the mustard?"

And a flash of irritation crosses God's face. But then he smiles and says, "Want Me to prove that promise? Try Me and see if I am God. Step out on that promise; jump up and down on it. It will hold; it's solid; I made it."

Thanks, Herm, for letting God speak through your welding, through the confidence you have in your workmanship.

Prayer Reflection

Mine: Master Welder, up above, how often You've taken this
       broken life of mine and fused it into respectability.
       Thanks 490 times! Sorry about that promise-question-
       ing. Really, You're the greatest!

                                    Yours truly,
                                    Your Welded Friend

Yours: _____

       _____

       _____

Therefore, if you are offering your gift at the altar and there remember that your brother has something against you, leave your gift there in front of the altar. First go and be reconciled to your brother; then come and offer your gift.

Matthew 5:23-24

3 TWENTY-FIVE YEARS LATE

A factory building on Richmond Street used to give me bad vibes every time I passed it. Now I feel good just thinking about it. Often today when we go by God whispers, "Well done, Bob." But there was a time when God and I had words about that building, or the man inside it.

God would say, "You need to stop in and see Tom."

But I always found an excuse. I was in a hurry; someone else was along; it was nearly closing time; Tom was probably busy. One day I did stop in, but Tom was out. I was glad, left hurriedly, happy to escape.

The next time God hassled me, I protested, "Lord, I did

stop in and he wasn't there."

Then I heard God speaking dryly, "Wouldn't it be reasonable to try again?"

I put it off, hoping God would forget. But He didn't. Nor could I.

It happened some twenty-five years ago. Tom would then have been only 11 or 12 years old. He was a mischievous lad, like many others. I was asked one Sunday to substitute as teacher in the Sunday school class where Tom was a member. In a poor mood for teaching that day, I had taken the class reluctantly. And it happened.

Tom wised off at the very beginning, and I was in no frame of mind for fun and games. I marched him outside, stood him in the hall, there to remain during the Sunday school hour. Severe punishment for a minor infraction, it proved that I was in charge. It wasn't right, but I did it.

Although twenty-five years had passed, what I had done gnawed away inside of me, always quickening as I passed the factory on Richmond Street. Now Tom was a prosperous businessman operating the factory. I recalled my cruelty and the hurt look on Tom's face when I put him out of the Sunday school class. God kept speaking to me about stopping in to straighten it out, but I found a barrel of excuses. God was patient, stayed on my back, reminded me of my duty. I said impatiently in return, "I know, I know!"

Then one day I screwed up the courage again and stopped. Tom was in. I was sorry; I was glad.

The receptionist called an inner office, and Tom opened the door to greet me. He was smiling, remembered me, invited me in. I wondered if he recalled the incident that had bugged me for twenty-five years.

We sat down, talked together about little things. I was tempted to tell him I just wanted to say hello and leave. But

God said "No" so loudly I thought Tom would surely hear.

So I told him about what happened years ago, his involvement, how driving by his factory was always bringing it to mind. Could he forgive me?

Tom sat across from me behind the spacious desk. Peck's bad boy had come a long way financially. His eyes studied me, a thin smile on the face. I wondered what was going through his mind. I suppose more than what he eventually shared.

Tom said kindly, "Bob, I don't remember that particular incident. I doubt if it affected me negatively. I've gotten along. I know I was a problem back then. But I think it was great of you to stop in, good for you, in fact necessary for you to do so." He kindly said nothing about the long delay.

I left shortly thereafter, still a bit ashamed, but a lot happier about the whole deal, much relieved.

I wasn't quite off the hook. God still had a word I needed to hear. "Bob, one thing does burn me about this. You waited twenty-five years to straighten this out. You're a schoolteacher. When a child refuses to follow your just directions, you accept a reasonable excuse, but not a string of them like you have been giving me for a quarter of a century. Do me a favor, will you? Either be a little more prompt in taking care of your own obligations, or back off from judging adolescents."

I needed the chewing out. Twenty-five years is too long to wait before you go to a brother and say, "Forgive me." Yet God had been patient with me for those twenty-five years, while I could not be patient with a 12-year-old boy for a Sunday school hour.

I am a schoolteacher. I know what it is to teach.

And I know what it is to be taught by God Himself. I have no quarrel with the blistering He gave me.

I am a better person because He laid it on me.

Yes, He laid it on, but when done, He took it off. Praise Him.

Prayer Reflection

Mine: Lord, I'm opening myself up when I make this request, but I want to make it. I'm nearing retirement age. There's more behind than there is ahead. Search the past years, remind me of my wrongs, the "Toms" I need to see. It will not take me twenty-five years. I promise.

—One Who Has Learned

Yours: _____

_____

_____

As Pharaoh approached, the Israelites . . . were terrified and cried out to the Lord. . . . Moses answered the people, "Do not be afraid. Stand firm and you will see the deliverance the Lord will bring you today."

Exodus 14:10, 13

4 GOD OF THE BROKEN PIECES

To be in a position of church leadership and make a wrong decision can be disastrous. Recently while serving on a committee, it happened to me. We were seeking consensus regarding a problem facing us. Time for reaching a solution to our dilemma was limited. It was a difficult problem to resolve. We were locked into taking a position of the moment.

Hindsight is often better than foresight, and our error soon became obvious to us and others in the church. In the process people were hurt.

For some time the matter weighed heavily upon me. It gave me a number of restless nights.

One night as I lay in bed, sleep not coming, I carried on a broken, one-sided conversation with God. "Lord," I complained, "You can do all things.... Why did You allow us to fail, to make a mess of this?... We wanted Your will to be done, You know that.... Why didn't You stop us?... Now look at what has happened.... It has hurt the church, Your body.... People are upset.... It's like everything is coming apart.... Around us lay the broken pieces."

Prayer is also God talking to us, and God was finally able to get a word in edgewise with me. He interrupted my groaning with the beautiful thought, "That's right, around you are the broken pieces. But you forget: I am the God of the broken pieces."

The churning inside me came to a halt. How true that message from the Almighty. In our humanity we had failed, but out of His divinity would come success. From the broken pieces our God would fashion a mosaic of loveliness for His glory.

I never cease to stop praising God for that sweet message His Spirit brought me that night.

Prayer Reflection

Mine: If I were perfect, Lord, I guess I wouldn't need You. If I were strong, I could walk alone. But I'm sinful, and I am weak. Thanks for forgiveness, for the songs you give in the night.

—Praising You

Yours: _____

_____

_____

One of the criminals who hung there hurled insults at him [Jesus]: "Aren't you the Christ? Save yourself and us!"

But the other criminal rebuked him, "Don't you fear God," he said, "since you are under the same sentence? We are punished justly, for we are getting what our deeds deserve, but this man has done nothing wrong"

Then he said, "Jesus, remember me when you come into your kingdom."

Jesus answered him, "I tell you the truth, today you will be with me in paradise."

Luke 23:39-43

5 COURAGE TO TURN AROUND

She shared with me the story of her grandfather's death. He had been the town character, a confirmed agnostic, a man who abused both his body and soul.

Upon his deathbed he was invited to accept Jesus Christ as his personal Savior. It was a dramatic, time-stopping scene.

Still feeling mentally alert, with supreme effort, the eighty-year-old dying man pulled himself to a sitting position. With a firm voice, he said, "There have never been any cowards in our family's history, and I don't propose to be the first."

With that he fell back upon his pillow and expired.

His dying defiance was noted throughout the community. Many persons commented that the man stood by his convictions. He died the way he had lived, defying on his deathbed the God he had denied all his life. Surely that was courage.

Driving home after Esther had told me the story, I thought to myself, "Yes, one would have to give the old man credit. There he was dying, probably conscious of the fact, yet he refused to yield. He was a man of convictions, courageous. I would have to agree with the opinion of his fellow townspeople." I nodded my head sadly, but honestly.

"A man of convictions, a courageous man?" God asked. "I disagree with both."

"How so, Lord?" I inquired.

"Well, in the first place, he's convictionless. He's an agnostic, doesn't believe in Me, has no intention of following me at all. So how could you call him a man of convictions? He is without convictions."

"A technicality, Lord," I answered. But I knew I had misused the word.

God snickered, then said, "As for 'courageous,' I would sooner call it 'stubborn.' I can find proof of what I mean by that in your own life. It takes courage, real courage to reverse yourself. You have said the same thing yourself. Remember about D-Day, compared to the letter you sent to the Commandant of the Ninth Naval District?

As I drove, I did some recalling. On June 6, 1944, the day the Allies invaded France, I was on a small landing craft at Utah Beach off the Normandy Beach of France. Within a few hours the first troops and tank destroyers from our landing boat struggled ashore. The shot and shell were still flying, demanding of me a certain level of courage.

Four years later, although still a member of the U.S. Naval Reserve and subject to recall, I notified my commanding officer at Great Lakes Naval Training Station that I would not accept a recall to active duty. Convinced that war was wrong, I no longer felt that I could serve. It was the time of the Korean conflict and my reversal of opinion was not a popular one. At that time I knew imprisonment was a possibility. It took more courage to write that letter and mail it than it did to participate in the D-Day landings in France during World War II.

Of this God was reminding me. I got the point, made the application.

Esther's grandfather simply died the way he lived. On his deathbed he had the opportunity to say, "I was wrong. For eighty years I have been wrong. I want to admit that error. I'm reversing myself."

True, he would have drawn the sneers of the villagers. They would have said that he chickened out. But to admit one's wrong, to stop, reverse the momentum of a lifetime and move in the opposite direction, ah, that takes a brand of courage that few are willing to declare. Esther's grandfather did not have it.

I knew God was right on both counts.

I have thought of a dozen turn-around incidents in my own life, and have seen it often in others. To say, "Look, I have been wrong; I'm sorry, forgive me," takes courage of a blue-ribbon variety.

To admit that you are wrong is tough. I know. Esther's grandfather does not. And between the two there is an eternity of difference.

Prayer Reflection

Mine: Lord, I plan no eleventh-hour switch-over. For nearly 50
years You have given me the courage with which to live,
and You will give me the courage with which to die.
Thanks in advance for holding my hand in that final
hour.

—No-Regrets Baker

Yours: _____

_____

_____

Let us then approach the throne of grace with confidence, so that we may receive mercy and find grace to help us in our time of need.

Hebrews 4:16

6 HEAVENLY COMPUTER SERVICE

The Sunday school lesson was based on the 23rd Psalm, six measly verses. I was to teach it to a large adult class. It was a psalm that everyone knew by heart. What new thing could I bring from it? How could such a familiar Scripture be profitable to go over again? How could it come alive to those of us who had known it since we were small children?

I thought about it for weeks, studied, read the commentaries, the lesson helps, complained to God. It was still the same beautiful 23rd Psalm, but oh so common. Most of the class members would know it by memory. Surely it was like a mine from which all the gold had been removed.

As the fatal Sunday drew near, I worried and fretted. I thought of getting sick.

Then one morning as I studied, alternating between sitting and stewing, pacing the room and pondering, I noticed the word "my" in the first verse: "The Lord is *my* shepherd."

I thought to myself, "That's nice, Lord. I'm glad You're 'my' shepherd. And millions of other people read that 'my' and rightly apply it to themselves. Having so many clients, patients, customers, subscribers, whatever You call us, must really keep You busy. I wonder how You keep track of us and work in regular appointments and emergency calls?" I sat down and wondered some more.

I dreamed. "Do you suppose God has some master computer up there in heaven?"

I envisioned God sitting at a master electronic console facing dozens of dials and gauges, with lights popping on and off, tiny beeps sounding, delicate bells jangling. Around Him sat thousands of angels at smaller computers, all linked by snakelike cables with the master one which God controlled. It was a busy scene I visioned, stretching for miles, an electronic masterpiece.

Zeroing in on one of the angel's computers, I saw to my amazement my own name and address above a tiny bulb that was flashing on and off like a call light outside a patient's room at the hospital. I watched the angel take note of it, manipulate a few switches, and adjust a dial. Soon I saw God speak into a microphone with a simple, "Yes?"

The angel with my name on his computer said, "Bob Baker is on the line. Shall I put him on hold?"

God smiled and said, "No, connect me direct. I know all about his problem." And I saw the Great One listening personally to my request for help on the Sunday school lesson.

He nodded, touched a button, and archangel Michael was immediately at His side.

God said, "I need someone to buzz down and help Bob Baker with a Sunday school lesson. He's all tied up in knots. Whose on call for him?"

Michael scanned a nearby TV screen and I saw my name appear, followed by "Enoch 4."

Michael said, "Enoch 4 is on call today. I might say, Lord, that I've gotten a lot of flack from some of the helpers we've sent to Baker. They say he's a real whiner." Michael paused, then to be sure that God understood, said, "That's 'whiner,' Lord, not 'winner.'"

God sighed. "Yes, I know. But he's one of My servants, and needs some help. So send Enoch 4 down to give him a lift."

Michael said, "10-4, Lord."

Then the whole scene faded out.

It was like a vision. Was that how it really was? Probably not.

But that personal touch, the confirmation that God was "*my*" Shepherd, treating me and 5-6 billion other people as if we are special, was a neat sweet feeling. God had His finger on me.

I knew that God would help me with the Sunday school lesson at Martinsburg, Pennsylvania.

And He did.

Prayer Reflection

Mine: I don't know how You do it, Lord, but you do. Thanks for Your personal service, individual attention, good computer readouts. You're the best deal I ever found.

—Cared for and Contented

Yours: _____

_____

_____

And we know that in all things God works for the good of those who love him, who have been called according to his purpose.

Romans 8:28

7 THE LADY AT THE WINDOW

Just before the plane was to leave O'Hare International Airport in Chicago, it became obvious that my teenage daughter, Rebecca, and I had not taken the assigned seats marked on our boarding pass. I was embarrassed because it was my fault. Rather than having the people involved change seats, the stewardess suggested we just remain where we were. I apologized to them.

On our side of the plane were three rows of seats. I was on the aisle, Rebecca in the middle, and an older lady by the window. Our companion seemed to be carrying a heavy burden. Her face appeared troubled, her eyes saddened.

Rebecca and I entered into conversation with her and eventually we learned of that concern. She was traveling to Colorado Springs, where her daughter lived. That daughter was to have a serious heart operation and our fellow traveler would be caring for her two small children during the next six weeks. As she felt our interest, the lady by the window shared freely of her fear about the operation, the responsibility that would be hers in that home.

As I listened, I thought of the "mistake" in seat reservations. Perhaps it was not a mistake. Had not God placed Rebecca and me there for such a time as this? Were we not a bit like Philip in the Bible, on the road from Jerusalem to Gaza, when the Ethiopian eunuch appeared, and God said, "Go to that chariot and stay near it?" I was becoming convinced that God wanted us to minister to this lady in some manner, but I wasn't sure how it should be done.

I breathed a silent request to God for guidance.

Immediately the answer came back, "Pray for this lady."

I answered, "I can do that at home, Lord."

God's reply was, "No, pray with her now. She has expressed her fear, her need is now, so meet that need at this moment."

I questioned the Lord further: "You mean pray aloud? On this crowded plane? Lord, I've already been embarrassed by my error in seating."

God said, "You asked for guidance, and I'm giving it to you. If you don't want to follow it, you shouldn't have asked Me for help."

That settled it. I leaned over to the lady by the window and said, "Would you like to have me pray for your daughter, for the surgeons, for yourself, that God might minister in and through all of you, give strength, leading, healing?"

Her eyes opened wide in pleasant surprise as she faced us, a happy smile replacing the worry. She said, "Oh, would you? I would be so grateful if you would."

I checked in once more with God: "Pray aloud?"

He said, "Of course. She expects it."

We joined hands, the three of us, and I forgot that we were on a plane flying over Midwestern United States, that curious passengers were around us. I just felt that I was where God wanted me to be at that very moment. So I prayed, softly, but aloud, for the lady at the window, her daughter in Colorado Springs, the surgeons that would operate next week.

When I was done, I looked into the lady's tear-brimmed eyes, noted Rebecca's trembling lip, and I knew that it was not a mistake that we sat in the wrong seats on that airplane.

It was all a part of God's plan and I rejoiced at my "mistake."

Prayer Reflection

Mine: It's another miracle! I sit in the wrong seat and it turns out to be the right seat. What seems stupid on my part turns out to be of heavenly design. Lord, I've a funny feeling that nothing happens to me without Your permission—and that's pretty neat.

Truly yours,
Bob

Yours: _____

_____

_____

God is not unjust; he will not forget your work and the love you have shown him as you have helped his people and continue to help them.

Hebrews 6:10

8 THE FURNACE WATCHER

When I start to make a snap estimate of a person, God reminds me of the furnace watcher. And I back up.

In 1959 I took a year off teaching and moved the family to East Lansing, Michigan, to study at Michigan State University. We attended a small, rural Mennonite Church some 35 miles north of the university. There I agreed to teach an adult Sunday school class.

After a few Sundays of teaching, I noticed I had a "dropout." One of the men who had been in the class for several Sundays no longer came. Although in church, he disappeared during the Sunday school hour.

Curious, I inquired around and found where he was hibernating. He was spending the Sunday school hour in the basement sitting by the coal-fired furnace.

His excuse for not attending class was, "This is an old furnace and needs a lot of attention."

It sounded like a weak excuse to me. In fact, I took it rather personally. The furnace-watching story seemed pretty flimsy.

Later that winter on a frigid Sunday morning as we were traveling to church, the old car that we were trying to nurse through our year of financial scarcity uttered a loud noise and gave up the ghost. The crankshaft had broken, the engine was ruined, and likewise our budget. It was a period of mourning.

The next time we attended the Bethel church (friends from East Lansing taking us), the furnace watcher came up to us and in a low unassuming voice had a request to make of me. He said, "I've done a lot of mechanical work. I repair and overhaul my own cars. I know where I can get a rebuilt engine for your car. Harold Zook and I would like to come down to the university tomorrow. We'll tow your car back up here, pull your old engine, and put in this good rebuilt one. You can pick it up next Sunday. Would you let us do that?"

I was deeply moved, ashamed. I had crossed this man off my list, had felt hurt because he chose meditating beside the furnace instead of my class. But he had not crossed me off his list. I found his action far more Christlike than my own. Perhaps, like Mary, he had chosen the better thing.

My car was repaired; it ran like new. Each time I drove it, God reminded me, "Please don't prejudge My children. Please don't scratch them off your pitifully small list."

And once as I crawled shamefacedly into the '53 Chevy,

God added for my special benefit: "Maybe, just maybe, sometimes a person can learn more about Me as he sits beside the furnace than he can by sitting in your class."

And God was so right.

Prayer Reflection

Mine: Lord, You remember that incident with the car the winter of 1960, and how Farol Bontrager, the furnace watcher, along with Harold bailed me out? What gracious servants of Yours they were! No degrees after their names, just love for You in their hearts. Unbeatable!

—Envious Me

Yours: _____

_____

_____

Jesus said, "It is not the healthy who need a doctor, but the sick. But go and learn what this means: 'I desire mercy, not sacrifice.' For I have not come to call the righteous, but sinners."

Matthew 9:12, 13

9 THE ADVANTAGE-TAKER

When my friend died, I felt pain. His death was quick, unexpected, and I thought needless. So with the pain there was bitterness.

My friend was retired, a man of great kindness, one who had reached out to help people. He gave freely of his limited money, counsel, time. But people took advantage of him, imposing upon him. And he let them do so.

In the middle of the winter, during a heavy snow, he was asked to help start a car for such an "advantage-taker." It was necessary to push the car through the snow for a short distance, and the exertion was too much. My friend suffered a heart attack and died instantly.

As I grieved, I also resented. I resented people who took advantage of others, who saw my friend as an easy mark, always good for a loan, for a ride, for an hour of his time.

At the funeral I brooded that it should not have been, that the man in the casket at the front of the church had left this life too early. We needed him, his wisdom, his understanding.

As I sat there, God said, "I know what you mean, Bob."

I was surprised. I feared that my thoughts weren't all Christian, that I should not be holding my friend's death against the kind of people who were never satisfied with what you did for them, who asked for more and more from you until there was nothing left to give. They sucked you dry. Now God was agreeing with me?

The service was progressing, but I was not hearing the minister. I was thinking my own sad thoughts, playing the same record over and over, always placing the death of my friend on the shoulders of people who only wanted to receive. They didn't care who they hurt in the process.

Then God began preaching a sermon just for me. "This death reminds Me of another. A Man whom I know so well lived here on earth for less than half the life of our friend up in front of the church. People took advantage of Him, clung to Him, asked Him to do this or that, continually begged for His services. They ran after Him, cried after Him, imposed upon Him.

"Sometimes He had to flee into the countryside just to get away for a few days of rest. In a way, He died of a broken heart also. He knew it was coming. He could have avoided it, but didn't.

"I think our friend today was similar. He didn't mind dying in the process of helping someone. Can you think of a better way to meet Me? How do you prefer to die, Bob, in action like these two I am talking about, or wasting away in some convalescent home?"

As always, God made His point so plain. I knew He was talking about His own Son. What He said made sense. God never held it against the sinners who caused Christ's death. Even His Son prayed for the thorn crowners, the nail pounders, the side piercers. So why should I blame others in the loss of my friend who really wanted to give himself to such people? That was his life.

The bitterness I had clustered to myself evaporated away. My friend Cleo died as he had lived—for others. Christ set the example, and Cleo followed. How could I knock it?

I wondered if I had the same mind-set, the same determination. Or would I hoard my remaining years, hours and minutes, jealously unto myself?

Prayer Reflection

Mine: I feel sort of crummy, Lord. I've been griping about some of your choice teachings. You said through Christ that You came to minister and help others. You told us that if we wanted to be someone, we had better be willing to pick up the towel and basin. I've been mouthing one thing, but living another. I need help.

—The Selfish One

Yours: _____

_____

_____

If we confess our sins, he is faithful and just and will forgive us our sins and purify us from all unrighteousness.

1 John 1:9

10 SIN IS LIKE POISON IVY

The old warning, "Leaflets three, let it be," never bothered me. Seemingly, I had a natural immunity to poison ivy.

Searching for wildflower and moss specimens, while hunting the fox squirrel or pursuing the sponge mushroom, I had tramped through miles and miles of woods, along numerous fencerows where poison ivy grew, and had never been infected with it in the slightest. It was a comforting feeling to have.

Sometimes I bragged that this pesky plant didn't bother me. I was safe and secure from its dreaded itch and weeping rash. So I thought.

About six years ago after a trip in the woods, small blisters appeared on my hands and between my fingers, accompanied by a dreadful itching and spreading, watery blisters. I went to the school nurse and inquired. With one quick look she said, "It looks like a typical case of poison ivy."

"But," I said, "I don't get poison ivy. I'm immune."

She replied dryly, "Maybe you think that you're immune, but if that's not poison ivy, then I'm not a registered nurse."

I checked further. She didn't have to worry about not being a registered nurse. Several infections during the succeeding years proved her right. My supposed immunity was gone.

God used that first-time infection with poison ivy to speak to me in a personal way. Older Christians such as I may feel secure, confident that certain temptations will never "infect" us. We could almost list the sins from which we are excused.

God informed me that is not so. One of Satan's oldest tricks is to encourage us to be overconfident. Then as we trust in our supposed immunity, the evil one strikes and we are infected.

We go to the Lord puzzled, asking, "What is it, Lord?"

And He says, "It is sin."

We reply, "But, Lord, I'm a mature Christian. This has never bothered me before. I thought I was immune to these sins of the flesh. How did this come about?"

And God replies sadly, "This I warned about in My Word: 'So, if you think you are standing firm, be careful that you don't fall.' No Christian has it made, none dare relax."

When I see poison ivy today, I give it a wide berth. I'm cautious about poison ivy. I want to take that same attitude toward temptation and sin of any kind. None of us is immune.

Prayer Reflection

Mine: Bluntly, frankly, Lord, I have sinned. Physician, I come to You for healing. I cannot stand this irritation, the scratching reminder of the sin I have committed. I am willing to take my medicine, for I desire to be made whole.

—Tired of Itching

Yours: _____

_____

_____

She [Zarephath widow] went away and did as Elijah had told her. So there was food every day for Elijah and for the woman and her family. For the jar of flour was not used up and the jug of oil did not run dry, in keeping with the word of the Lord spoken by Elijah.

1 Kings 17:15, 16

11 GOD, MY BATTERY SPECIALIST

When the chorister at Riverside Mennonite Church near Turner, Michigan, announced her first song, I almost smiled out loud. The song was "Great Is Thy Faithfulness." The previous day God had tested me, then metered out to me just the right amount of mercy I needed. He proved His sufficiency. He showed that He too could be Mr. Goodwrench. He understood car batteries.

On Saturday, the day of my testing, I was driving 250 miles northward to Turner, Michigan, for a weekend speaking appointment. About 75 miles out of Elkhart, Indiana, the alternator warning light came on red, glaring at me from

the dashboard of the little Japanese Subaru I was driving.
No longer would it charge my battery. Ouch. I was too far
from home to turn back and exchange cars, too far from
Turner to take a chance.

Could I get it fixed that Saturday afternoon along the
way?

Each place I stopped the mechanics were either off duty
or drew back in horror at the thought of working on such a
strange car. When I explained my problem, they just smiled
and said, "You might make it, if your battery is strong
enough."

There was no help from man, so I tried God. I explained
the situation in detail, emphasizing that I was giving up a
weekend for Him. God said, "I can handle it." But He gave
no details, and I wanted specifics.

Did God know that this was a used car, that the battery
was the original—probably four years old? Yes, He knew
that.

Should I stop at Lansing to buy another battery and carry
it along as a spare? God reminded me of my cash flow outward and I knew it was a dumb question. I worried my way
northward, using nothing electrical if I could keep from it,
hurrying, nursing my worries. The red light still stared at
me. I am no mechanic, but the battery could only be getting
weaker. Was God really with me on U.S. 69 or had I just
been "hearing things"?

Finally I arrived at Turner. My host for the weekend was
to be Leon Stutzman and I knew the road on which he lived.
I decided to stop at the first house on that road and ask for
further directions. When I pulled in, I forgot and shut off
the ignition. I could be in trouble.

The lady at the house wore a Mennonite prayer veiling. I
felt good. At least I was among friends, my people. Did she

know where the Stutzmans lived? She smiled and pointed to the next small farm a few hundred yards down the road. I laughed in relief, explaining my car's electrical problems.

When I got back in the car and turned the ignition key, the battery delivered its last trickle of juice. The motor barely grunted. I tried again. Total silence.

Then God whispered to me, with a smile, "Do you think you can handle it from here?" I grinned.

My new friends gathered around the car and we rejoiced at how faithful God had been. With jumper cables we started the Subaru. At the Stutzmans I found further help— a battery charger and mechanical aid denied me on the way up. Like the widow's oil and her meal, God measured out sufficient current for my need.

No wonder chorister Twila Swartz led that particular song. The whole weekend was God pleading, "Trust me."

I'll try, Lord: I promise.

Prayer Reflection

Mine: Father, You never cease to amaze me. You are so versatile. You minister to my car, my bank account, my lawn, my house—you name it. You can handle it. You cover the yellow pages. You are everything to me.

—Cared for by God Himself

Yours: _____

_____

_____

With the tongue we praise our Lord and Father, and with it we curse men, who have been made in God's likeness. Out of the same mouth come praise and cursing. My brothers, this should not be.

James 3:9, 10

12 THE ZACCHAEUS FORMULA

The gloves were leather with a special insulated lining. I really liked them and had carefully placed my name and address inside each cuff. If I ever lost them, I wanted them returned.

I did lose them in the immediate Elkhart area. No letter or telephone call came to my home, no newspaper ad appeared announcing that my gloves were found. In my mind I saw them found, appropriated. Someone picked up those gloves and said, "Finders keepers." My name had been inked out. It was a form of stealing.

Several times in talking to people I mentioned the glove

incident. It was a good illustration of declining morals, each person looking out for himself, the disappearance of honesty.

Then just before Christmas I cleaned out the small luggage shelf in the car. It's where we keep the Kleenex box and other miscellaneous items. Behind the tissues, pressed against the back of the compartment, were my "lost," my "stolen" gloves.

In a flash I recalled how I had placed them in that compartment myself. I remembered the very day, the exact occasion when I had done it. Then I had promptly forgotten about it until now.

I was delighted at my discovery. I said with happiness, naturally, fervently, "Thank you, Lord, thank you!"

And God replied, I thought a bit coldly, "You're welcome."

I wondered at His coolness and asked about it.

God said, "I was just wondering about how many times you have bad-mouthed people for 'finding' your gloves and not returning them."

I said humbly, "Maybe two or three times. I'm sorry about that. But what can I do about that now?"

He told me how He wanted the account to be squared away. He called it "the Zacchaeus way." Zacchaeus had said, "If I have cheated anybody out of anything, I will pay back four times the amount." So God suggested that my "false accusations" against my fellowmen be replaced fourfold by "good accusations."

Two or three times I had borne false witness. I wondered which number I should multiply by four.

As if reading my mind, God advised, "Bob, let's use the three. Let's make it twelve times, an even dozen times you are to praise your fellowmen."

Then He added, "And please keep track of it. Mark it

down. I don't want you to forget it like your gloves."

I protested that was legalism, but He explained again that legalism was for those who could not handle the way of His Son, to love both God and neighbor as oneself.

That's why I carry in my wallet a little score card. I started today and already I have two marks on it. When I get ten more, I may have established a good habit and eliminated a bad one.

Prayer Reflection

Mine: Glove Finder, I want one thing clear. You hear me protest, even resist at times, because of what You say to me. Please don't stop talking to me because I seem negative and resentful. When I think it over, I always see that You were right and I was wrong. I hate to be corrected, but I sure need to be.

—Stubborn

Yours: _____

_____

_____

When you pass through the waters, I will be with you; and when you pass through the rivers, they will not sweep over you. When you walk through the fire, you will not be burned; the flames will not set you ablaze. For I am the Lord, your God.... You are precious and honored in my sight ... because I love you.... Do not be afraid, for I am with you.

Isaiah 43:2-5

13 GOD'S RADAR SCREEN

As we crossed northern Indiana the pilot came on the plane's intercom. He informed us that it would be necessary to divert our course somewhat because of thunderstorms. Our estimated arrival time at O'Hare Airport in Chicago would be delayed, perhaps by fifteen minutes.

No sweat for me since I had nearly two hours layover time before my connecting flight left for South Bend.

But the fifteen minutes extended to half an hour. We flew through thick gray clouds, lightning flashing in the not-too-far distance.

Again our pilot briefed us. Two of the landing strips at

O'Hare had been put out of commission by the storm and we would be further delayed. Then he added, "We are in a stack of three planes, maintaining our position about 60 miles southwest of Chicago. We expect clearance for landing before long." Pilots are always optimistic.

As we continued to circle, the plane conversation grew quieter. Outside the lightning continued, grayness streamed by. As I sat by the window, I peered out and down. I saw nothing. I pictured the officers in the cabin ahead flying on instruments, moving at the beck and call of the air-control directors in the tower at O'Hare north of us.

I must confess that disturbing thoughts entered my mind. Would diminishing fuel supplies send us to some other airport? Could the pilot of this or another plane, a radar operator below, err and place two airships on a collision course?

But I shook off the feeling. Instruments were reliable, radar screens plotted us, pilots were experienced. We were being viewed, followed, and checked by alert air-control people. I relaxed and waited, God switching my thoughts.

I pictured God in some giant control tower, every day and every night having me and billions of other people on His giant radar screen, angels operating smaller units, computers humming, everything linked together in one gigantic electronic complex.

God was carefully monitoring my position, as well as the lives of billions of other people, always ready through the Holy Spirit or angelic messengers to send me course-changing information so I would miss a collision with Satan, a sin storm in my path, the temptation to fly too low or too high.

I thought of God watching over me as I flew through the gray clouds of depression, bringing me safely through into heavenly sunlight, easing each air pocket of despair, deflecting sin bolts the evil one hurled at me. God knew and cared all about me. I was in good hands.

Miles above Illinois I praised God that I was always on His radar screen. His traffic control in my life was the one that really counted.

Prayer Reflection

Mine: When planes crash, they look for mechanical failure or pilot error. With You at the controls, Lord, I worry about neither. There's not a landing You can't make, not a failure You can't override. You can pilot me anytime, anyplace.

—Secure in You

Yours: _____

_____

_____

He put a new song in my mouth, a hymn of praise to our God. Many will see and fear and put their trust in the Lord.

Psalm 40:3

14 THE BICYCLE SONG

Riding a bicycle to school is often a therapeutic, spiritual exercise for me. It's like a tonic. Especially in the mornings, God seems very close.

During the past year or so, He has given me a song that I as a monotone can sing as I ride without worrying if I am offending others. God is never offended. My monotone is not monotonous to Him. This morning He gave me another verse to that song, one that I needed, that brought me much joy. After we went over it several times God said, "Share it with others, Bob."

But I protested that it was our song, and besides, it was so simple, and I wasn't even sure if the meter was right. I always have lots of reasons to remain selfish.

In reply He said, "What I have helped you to create is of worth. You need not be ashamed of it. You should not be selfish with it. I will use it to bless someone."

So I monotoned through our song as I continued to school, all the verses I could remember.

> When your days seem dark and gray,
> When it seems so hard to pray,
> Say, "Praise the Lord," say, "Praise the Lord."

> When your days have been so long,
> When it seems you've lost your song,
> Say, "Praise the Lord," say, "Praise the Lord."

> When your burdens weigh you down,
> Don't forget you wear a crown,
> Say, "Praise the Lord," say, "Praise the Lord."

Then the new verse, the one He gave me this morning:

> When your life is dry and sour
> You must claim the Jesus power,
> Say, "Praise the Lord," say, "Praise the Lord."

Then I went through the chorus a couple of times:

> It is the answer, it is the answer,
> Placing you in sweet accord.

I'm certain that it must seem strange to one musically inclined that a song could be sung set to a single note of music. But God and I like that song.

And God said, "Share it."

So I did.

Prayer Reflection

Mine: Dear Lord, moments alone with You are precious, price-
        less. I tend to be jealous of them, of You. Teach me to
        share those tender moments with others. You have
        enough love for all of us.

                                        —The Monotoner

Yours: _____

_____

_____

Do not let your hearts be troubled. Trust in God; trust also in me. In my Father's house are many rooms; if it were not so, I would have told you. I am going there to prepare a place for you. And if I go and prepare a place for you, I will come back and take you to be with me that you also may be where I am.

John 14:1-3

15 FUNERAL ARRANGEMENTS

The casket manufacturer was firm in speech, yet gentle, as he talked about the merits of the burial container. He could absolutely guarantee that, with a proper vault, the casket would always protect the loved one within. Water could not enter that beautiful resting chamber. He promised reverently that no moisture would ever touch the cloth or the body.

As I listened, I'm afraid my eyes glazed over. I thought of other things, my mind an eternity away. What use had I for this body after death? Although it had given me good service for these 60 years, would I be using it in heaven?

Somehow, I thought that God had a new, a better model waiting for me.

But if He didn't, if He chose to restore and reconstruct this present flesh into a perfect body, I cared not. I knew this—a bit of moisture could not stop any recreative process He might intend to use. He began mankind with a handful of dust and I was convinced He would do fine with whatever contents remained in the box ten years from now, or a hundred, a thousand years in the future.

If I am disfigured at death, or ravaged by disease down to half my regular weight, I knew that He would know me.

Forty-eight years ago I made the most important funeral arrangement in the world. I arranged with God for an eternity of care.

My casket, simple or complex, wooden or metal, loosely fitted or hermetically sealed, will not matter. I'll not be there.

Prayer Reflection

Mine: Father, I've nothing against funeral directors. Some are my Christian brothers, dear friends. It's just that You have made preparations that take precedent over theirs. At death, let them make me presentable to my friends, but thanks to Your dear Son, I've been made presentable to You many years ago!

Yours forever,
Bob

Yours: _____

_____

_____

You are the light of the world. A city on a hill cannot be hidden. Neither do people light a lamp and put it under a bowl. Instead they put it on its stand, and it gives light to everyone in the house. In the same way, let your light shine before men, that they may see your good deeds and praise your Father in heaven.

Matthew 5:14-16

16 LIGHT IS COSTLY

I sat in the Belmont Mennonite Church and listened to Dick Lehman, worship leader, as he led our thinking about "light" in preparation for the sermon on that subject. He referred to the burning candles, a part of the worship decor, and commented about Jesus as the light of the world.

But God had something special for me there that morning, something that came spinning out of Dick's beginning thoughts. Based on my science background, God continued the lesson.

Did people consider what the light was costing the candle?

The candle's tallow, its carbon and hydrogen compounds, were rising up the wick by capillary attraction, there to vaporize, to burn, to become water vapor, carbon dioxide, to be consumed, finished as tallow.

I thought of other light sources, how each time something "pays the price" for light produced. On the sun, the hydrogen becomes helium, losing some of its mass. In the incandescent light bulb, the tungsten filament slowly deteriorates. In the campfire, the wood turns to ashes.

I recalled what happens when a solid becomes hot enough to glow, to become incandescent. As electrons circle in tiny orbits, they rise to higher levels, but almost immediately fall back into their original orbit. Yet as they fall, they give off the energy that had been imparted to them in photons of visible light.

The presence of light means that something has changed, been given up, used, surrendered, reduced to a simpler and humbler form of matter, accepted a lower position. Matter is not destroyed, but it is changed.

How true this is in the spiritual life also. When God imparts His spiritual energy to me, I rise to a higher level. But He wants me to fall back toward Him for fresh input. And each time I fall back to the Nucleus of my life, I give off light. But if I glory alone in my new orbit, refuse to drop back, to be "humbled" and dependent upon Him, then I give off no light.

Where does it end? That's the thriller. It never does. Each time I fall back into His arms, the everlasting arms, I am charged afresh, rising to new orbits of grace, finding new areas for sharing. As I give of myself, decreasing so others may increase, always I know that there is an energy source waiting below to fill me anew, to kick me up to a higher orbit.

It's an energy source spelled with capital letters, uncontrolled by OPEC. Long after the fossil fuels are gone, He will be there.

Prayer Reflection

Mine: Lord, You light up my life. If I shine, it's because of You. One of the nicest things about glowing is knowing that I am returning to You for fresh charging, new enabling.
—One of Your Sunbeams

Yours: _____

_____

_____

If you, then, though you are evil, know how to give good gifts to your children, how much more will your Father in heaven give good gifts to those who ask him!

Matthew 7:11

17 CONTENT WITH SECOND BEST

Two years ago I noticed my black topcoat was frayed at the cuffs, becoming rather threadbare, so I purchased for several dollars another nice black one at a used clothing store. It was nearly new and showed little sign of wear.

During the past summer my wife sent the new purchase to the dry cleaners. It was returned, fresh and neat. She placed the coat in the closet. Gradually through the succeeding weeks it worked itself to the rear behind the other garments.

Last fall, with the arrival of the first chilly weather, I absentmindedly pulled out the frayed and tattered one that should have been discarded, but hadn't been. I completely forgot about the newer purchase, and it remained hidden behind an assortment of other clothing.

Through Christmas I wore the old one, a bit ashamed of the poor appearance it made, resolving that I must get to the budget shop and replace the relic.

Then one day in sorting through the closet, I found the topcoat that had been brought back from the dry cleaners. It was still wrapped in its plastic garment bag.

In surprise I told my wife of my discovery.

She smiled and said, "I wondered why you didn't wear it, but I figured you were hoping to get a little more mileage out of the old one." I am noted in the family for my economy.

Later as I was reading from the Bible, chapter 3 of the Book of Colossians, I was reminded again of how the Christian should put off anger, wrath, filthy communication, and put on kindness, long-suffering, and other godly characteristics. God reminded me at that time of the forgotten coat. He said, "Bob, I have so many new beautiful things for each Christian, but some of you persist in hanging onto and wearing the seedy, tacky 'garments' that I wanted you to put off and discard long ago. Why do you do that, Bob?"

I confessed to Him it was habit, and asked Him to kick me the next time I as a Christian wore a sinner's garment.

God promised He would do that very thing.

Prayer Reflection

Mine: Supplier of all my needs, why do I go around in the piti-
ful rags of unbelief when You have stocked my wardrobe
with garments so lovely they defy description? Why do I
dress like a spiritual bum while tailored garments of
glory hang unused nearby?

—Color Me Stupid

Yours: _____

_____

_____

How great is the love the Father has lavished on us, that we should be called children of God! And that is what we are!

1 John 3:1

18 GOD'S CONSUMING LOVE

When it finally sank in, I trembled. I had guessed at my condition, questioned my symptoms, but never before had I faced up to what might actually be growing inside me. Now it was obvious; the truth could not be denied. I was totally infected with God's love. The knowledge overwhelmed me. I would never be the same again. My ailment had only one outcome.

How strange the occasion when the moment of truth came booming in. I was driving down the highway on a beautiful summer day when I accepted the fact. For a moment I drove unconsciously, the tears streaming down my face, my heart pounding. Then I realized what was happening—the danger involved. I pulled onto the berm of the road and came to a shaky stop. I sat there with bowed head. "Why me, Lord? What have I done to deserve this?"

When had it happened? When had my body been invaded, the change begun, division and multiplication taken place, spreading throughout, producing a condition that only a miracle could undo?

Why didn't I realize before what was happening? Why didn't I see the signs along the way, the hints of changes that were taking place? Perhaps I had been too busy.

Then I raised my tear-drenched face and looked around. I saw the blue sky glistening, the golden wheat waving in the field beside the road. God had not failed me. He was good. Through my tears I thanked Him for my present condition.

For years I had been a Christian and failed to realize that I had been so totally infected with God's love. Through Bible study, prayer, and the church that love virus had bloomed inside me, divided, multiplied, now possessed me. No man could pry me from the Father's hand.

Such a beautiful "ailment," such a lovely "disease." How I rejoiced in my "infection" and the prognosis of this "disorder." I could not be cured of God's love. I was hopelessly afflicted.

I started the car, eased out into the traffic, basking in spiritual ecstasy because of the truth the Holy Spirit had brought to me. When God's love truly invades us, we must succumb to it.

There is no cure for God's love.

Prayer Reflection

Mine: Lord of life, Lord of love, I can neither measure nor understand Your love to me. But, I'll tell You, I sure do enjoy it! Keep it coming.

—Thankful Me

Yours: _____

_____

_____

They also will answer, "Lord, when did we see you hungry or
thirsty or a stranger or needing clothes or sick or in prison, and did
not help you?" He will reply, "I tell you the truth, whatever you
did not do for one of the least of these, you did not do for me."

Matthew 25:44, 45

19 THE DETOUR

He attended our church, and I think it would be fair to say
that he took advantage of fellow members. He borrowed
money and possessions and asked favors, sometimes returning what he borrowed, sometimes not. School came hard for
him. He ran around with the wrong crowd and found it difficult to stick to any job. He caused us some heartache.

Yet I liked him. We all did.

Still, when we met, when he called me, I was always on
the alert, wondering, "Now, what does he want?" True,
sometimes he just talked, but I always feared that I would
hear another request. So it went year after year.

Now my friend is gone, never to return to this earth. He died young. And I have some regrets—especially one—one in which God spoke clearly and precisely to me. God laid it on the line, censored me, and I have nothing to say in any real defense of my action, except the words with which I keep sending to Him again and again, penitent words, "Lord, I'm sorry." God always hears, but I feel bad because some of those "I'm sorrys" come because of sins of commission, not omission. I made the decisions myself, and they were wrong. I had time to think about it, but made the wrong choice. I counted the cost and refused to pay it. I chose not to walk the second mile Jesus talks about in Matthew 5:41. I failed my young friend.

He was on the highway outside Goshen, Indiana, hitchhiking a ride in the opposite direction in which I was going. For a moment I thought of stopping, turning around, taking him to his destination.

But I was on my way to an appointment. I had a schedule to keep. Who knew how far he wanted to go, how long it would take?

So I waved and went on. He would understand. If I had been going his way, I would have stopped. Someone else would pick him up. Besides, my friend had quit several jobs. He could have had his own car easily by now if he had worked and saved his money. He could hardly expect me to detour to supply his needs.

Now he is gone and I don't have to worry about him.

But I do.

Several months ago his name flashed into my mind. I recalled him so plainly standing there on the highway berm, the friendly wave, the pleasant smile as I went past in the opposite direction that he was traveling. He understood—I thought. Then came God with a painful comparison.

"Some years ago I saw you, Bob, on life's highway, trying to hitchhike a ride, trying to reach a destination. You were going in the opposite direction from the way I was traveling. I was busy and thought of passing you by. I wondered if you were worth picking up. I called My Son over and said, 'Bob Baker's down there with arm upraised asking for help, going in the wrong direction. There are others down there too, more to come, millions of them, but right now I see Bob Baker. Would you go?' "

I knew Christ's answer. He came to pick me up. If I had been the only one, He still would have come. That's not conceit on my part; that's love on His part.

That's why I feel bad about my young friend. The day he asked for help, I said, "No." Now he will bother me no more.

And I wish so much he could.

Prayer Reflection

Mine: Jesus, You picked me up, when I was going the wrong direction. You detoured, stopped, invited me to ride with You. I didn't do that with my friend. I left him standing there, arm upraised, pleading for a lift. But I had a schedule to keep. Forgive me, Brad; forgive me, Lord. I'm really sorry.

—Unworthy Me

Yours: _____

_____

_____

"I, even I, am he who blots out your transgressions, for my own sake, and remembers your sins no more."

Isaiah 43:25

20 THE CONFESSOR

It was after 10:00 p.m. one Sunday night when the phone rang at our home. A youthful voice asked if I was the teacher who taught in the Elkhart school system. And I said, "Yes."

My caller introduced herself and asked if I remembered her as a student in my summer biology course of several years back. Of course, I remembered Jane, a quiet hardworking young lady.

Jane said to me in a trembling voice, "Mr. Baker, I've just come from a service at our church. I rededicated my life to God. Now I must tell you something . . . ." There was hesitation, and I heard her say, "I'm afraid I'm going to cry."

For a moment I listened to her quiet sobbing, wondering what this was all about. Then she regained her composure and continued.

"Mr. Baker," Jane said, "on the final examination in your class, I cheated. I wanted so much to get a "B" in that course. I'm sorry, but I cheated." More hesitation.

Then words again, words that weighed a ton. "Mr. Baker, I've talked this over with our pastor. We agreed that I should call you. I want you to know that if you think you should go to the central office and change my grade to a failing one, it's all right with me."

I said, "Jane, aren't you a senior? Don't you graduate in June?"

The soft, but firm answer came back, "Yes." She had counted the cost.

I did some rapid thinking. The examination was important, but not that important. By her confession she had just passed a more difficult test. I knew what I must do.

Gently I said, "Jane, you did the wrong thing that summer. You did the right thing tonight when you confessed. It's all right. Your action tonight reveals to me that you have learned a valuable lesson about life. Biology is a study of life. Your A plus tonight in the little examination you have just taken should balance out that biology exam." I knew I was playing God, but I know too that He expects us to be God-like.

There was a moment of silence, then the testimony, "Mr. Baker, you don't know how good I feel."

And I said back, "Jane, you don't know how good I feel. Good night, and God bless you."

Two people hung up their phones. I know that both of us sat there and cried, thanking God for the healing that always follows confession and forgiveness.

Prayer Reflection

Mine: It's me, Lord, old sinful Baker. The good front I put on for people gets peeled away when I stand before You. Like Jane, I'm calling You up to tell you of my latest sin. Like her, I'm not proud of it. Please forgive me.

—Smudged

Yours: _____

_____

_____

The young man said, "What do I still lack?" Jesus answered, "If you want to be perfect, go, sell your possessions and give to the poor, and you will have treasure in heaven. Then come, follow me."

Matthew 19:20, 21

21 SPARKING CHRISTIANS

My wife returned from an auction sale with a box of miscellaneous items that included two electric razors. Since my own shaver was rather ancient and faltering, I was happy with her purchase.

When I plugged it in, the first razor ran like a charm. But the second one remained silent, not a "buzz" from it. As I sat there at the kitchen table, I thought to myself, "Well, getting the one shaver is still a bargain, but I wish the other one would run also." I gave it a little shake, and to my surprise it ran for a fraction of a second. I repeated the action; again it ran briefly.

I like to tinker so I took the shaver cover off, exposed the motor, plugged it in again, watching as I shook it.

I made an interesting discovery. When it ran for that brief instant, a tiny spark flickered where a delicate spring touched a piece of metal. On the opposite side of the motor was another spring, identical in shape and position to the one that was sparking. Only it didn't touch the metal plate, nor was it sparking.

I took a small screwdriver with an insulated handle and gently lifted the touching spring from the metal. Immediately the razor burst into a constant, satisfying hum. I bent the spring permanently away from the metal and the razor ran perfectly. The sparking was gone. The electrical short had been eliminated.

But still more important to me was the thought that came later. Some Christians do not operate smoothly. They function spasmodically and run only when shaken. Some imperfection in their life causes them to short out. Some place in their spiritual structure there is a bent wire, a point were they are touching the world, draining spiritual energy from their life, preventing them from running for the Lord.

I wonder what could happen if every Christian in this world operated for just twenty-four hours at full capacity? Surely the tremendous pulse of spiritual power that would surge through the world would shake many a sinner into the kingdom.

But instead we sputter and spark, faint and falter, stumble and stall, in our witness and walk for God.

It's kind of sad.

Prayer Reflection

Mine: Lord, when I'm not running right, shake me, find my
trouble, then bend me so I function as I should. I want
to run for You.

—Willing, but Weak

Yours: _____

_____

_____

Jesus looked at them and said, "With man this is impossible, but with God all things are possible."

Matthew 19:26

22 THE IMPOSSIBLE

She called at 8:00 on a Thursday evening. She wanted me to come to her brother's funeral in Glendive, Montana. The funeral was to be on Saturday morning and I needed to be back in Elkhart, Indiana, by Sunday noon for an appointment of long-standing.

As Vaughn asked me to participate in the funeral, I calculated the chances of getting a substitute for my teaching position on Friday, a plane reservation that would get me to Montana on time and back here on time. The first was possible, the second, "Wow!" The odds against that were phenomenal.

I told Vaughn Kauffman in Montana, "You know I'd come if I could, but I'm afraid you're asking the impossible. Menno Travel of Goshen, who would check out the schedule possibilities for me, is closed for the day. I'll try, Vaughn, but don't count on it."

Vaughn, a young lady of 22 with a deep faith in God, gently replied, "You try, Bob, and I'll be praying that you make it."

I hung up in despair thinking, "Vaughn, you're dreaming. . . . Lord, if You were me, where would You start?"

And He said, "If I were you, I would start with that travel agency in the shopping mall. They're still open."

I had forgotten about them, having depended on Menno Travel in the past.

I quickly called the agency at the mall and explained my needs. The agent whistled as he comprehended the quickness and tightness of my demands.

"I know it's Thursday night and that the weekend is a busy time," I said. "I'll leave tomorrow if necessary. Just get me there for the funeral at 10:00 Saturday morning, and don't forget the Sunday deadline in getting back."

The travel agent's doubt came right over the telephone wire and merged with mine, merged in complete agreement. I didn't tell him that Vaughn was praying for the impossible, acting as if there was nothing to it.

Meanwhile I called my assistant principal and explained the situation. He gave his blessing. If the plane reservation came through (which he doubted), they would find a substitute.

In twenty minutes the phone rang. It was the travel agent at the mall. He said calmly. "We have your plane reservation to Montana."

I couldn't believe it. I asked about departure time, arrival time, returning time. Everything fit into the necessary time frame. The agent said, "We were fortunate. Things just seemed to work out."

It was another one of those things that shouldn't have happened, but did.

I have often thought of that dramatic weekend, the closeness, but the exactness with which things worked out. Coming back from Chicago's O'Hare, there was a brief delay involving a small commuter plane. I wondered if God was going to slip up after all and blow my schedule at the end. But the plane problem was solved. God had fit all the pieces of the jigsaw puzzle together nicely.

I can still hear Vaughn's soft voice saying with confidence, "Bob, I'll be praying that you make it." There was no doubt in her words, only quiet confidence.

I never fail to be amazed when I see and hear of how God moves the mountains, tossing them into the midst of the seas.

Prayer Reflection

Mine: Top Man, I've surely got that disciple Thomas beat all hollow in this matter of doubting. Put me in the *Guinness Book of Records*. I keep saying, "This can't happen," but it does. You proved me wrong again. And thanks for doing so.

—Thomas Baker

Yours: _____

_____

_____

I [Jesus] tell you the truth, anyone who has faith in me, will do what I have been doing. He will do even greater things than these, because I am going to the Father.

John 14:12

23 THE GOD OF ELIJAH

The church brother shook his head at my story. I had just told him with excitement about what I called "my little miracle." The ailing electrical system on my car collapsed completely, but only at the end of a long journey, and after I had safely reached my destination. During the trip I had been praying that I could "make it" in spite of alternator failure. And I had. So, in the presence of my brother, I had praised God for extending the life of my battery.

The smiling one said, "Bob, that was no miracle, small or large. That was simply a routine mechanical problem, a cause-and-effect relationship. The timing was just a happenstance. You lucked out. You can't make a miracle out of a battery conking out at a convenient time."

And his observation depressed me.

Was it true that what I had claimed as an answer to prayer was nothing more than luck, fate, or chance? For several days his comments kept coming to my mind, and each time I felt the gray clouds of despondency swirl around me.

Then one morning on the way to school, the phrase, "Where now is the Lord, the God of Elijah?" flashed into my questioning mind. These were the words of Prophet Elisha in 2 Kings 2:14 when he smote and separated the Jordan River with Elijah's mantle.

When I arrived at school, I hurriedly took a Bible and checked out "the Lord, the God of Elijah" in 1 Kings 17. The account tells of the widow of Zarephath who used her last handful of meal, and the last drops of her oil, to make Elijah a cake. I read with a thrill, verse 16: "For the jar of flour was not used up and the jug of oil did not run dry." That was what the God of Elijah had done.

The cloud lifted. My friend had a right to his opinion, but God had confirmed to me my right to claim a miniature miracle, to feel that the "electrical energy wasted not, neither did the battery fail" in my car.

God said to me, "Bob, there have been plenty of times when I worked through you and you took the credit. You gave me none of the glory. Like the nine lepers My Son healed, you went merrily on your way. I work through the natural, and I work through the supernatural. I want you to bring all of your problems to Me, and I, the God of Elijah, will be your God also. Thanking Me for what others may classify as simply 'the way things worked out' can make up for your negligence and shortsightedness in the past, your failure to see Me at work in your life. You cannot come to

Me too often with your praise."

I thanked the God of Elijah again for the battery that failed not.

Prayer Reflection

Mine: Some may think I'm becoming senile in my old age, turning from a cause-and-effect religion to a simple childlike faith in You. But is there any other way into the kingdom than by becoming like one of those little ones You held in your arms 2,000 years ago?

—Simpleminded Me

Yours: _____

_____

_____

Blessed are the merciful, for they will be shown mercy.
Matthew 5:7

24 HANG IN, OR HANG IT UP?

Several years ago I tried a new area of work. I did it at a time when the pressures from other duties were extremely strong, perhaps the greatest in some 40 years of church work.

I survived the effort which involved working with a number of young people. An evaluation form was required from each participant in which helpful criticism was solicited from all. There were the usual comments: good, neutral, indifferent.

But among the evaluations were two that I remember with great clarity. One person thanked me and said, "I think you should try this again." Translated, that meant, "You did not do so well, but I think you can improve, so don't let it get you down. Hang in there."

The other evaluation said, "I don't think you should ever try this again. You don't have the academics for success on this level of work." That hardly needed a translation, saying rather plainly, flatly, "You have not only failed, but I see no hope for you, since you have neither the background nor intelligence to succeed in this area. Hang it up."

The two critics were of the same age, both highly intelligent. Both suggested failure on my part. The one offered hope, the other did not. I confess the latter was depressing. The matter kept coming back to me—the work, the evaluation. I reviewed them both. I talked to God about it.

"Lord, You know how it was. Under the circumstances I don't see how I could have done any better. There were the four weekend meetings during the six weeks that went before, all intense, all out of state. There was the burden of school, of home, of writing. And I tried. You remember the hours spent in preparation, hours stolen from other work. I did involve resource people in the effort. I counted on them to help fill in the cracks."

God replied, "No need to apologize. I remember. I understood. I never criticized you."

But I injected, "You allowed this criticism and from one of your children."

"Bob, let's leave the evaluator out of this. That's between Him and me, and I think I can handle it. I'm concerned about what you learn from this experience.

"What you do with failure is up to you. Your critics suggest at least two options: You can grit your teeth and try again, or you can fold up, feel sorry for yourself, withdraw.

"But there's something more. You can learn something about your own evaluations. I've heard you refer to some of your students at school as 'zeroes,' another way of saying 'hopeless.' True, you never said that to the student, but you did in talking to other teachers. No one is a 'zero,' Bob, no one. Point number 1.

"And point number 2? Coming up. I recall times when you have made home calls on students, talked with them after school, took time to read their cumulative records, talked to the counselors about them, trying to get inside their 'skin.' And every time you did, you softened your criticism, raised your evaluation. You said there was more to a child than what you saw in the classroom. You stretched your grading scale and gave a child hope."

Then God went silent. I guess He knew I needed time for the words to inch in. Failure could be a stepping stone, a learning experience. And if so, was it a failure? In a negative evaluation you can offer hope, or you can be jealous of academic standards and draw hard, firm, uncrossable lines.

Finally I said, "Lord, did I have to have this painful lesson in order to learn what You have just taught me?"

Quick and quiet came the answer, "You did."

It doesn't mean that I rule out failing a student, that I have become a "yes" man. It simply means that before I give a negative criticism, I had better walk with that person and try to see the world through his eyes.

Sometimes what I see changes my mind.

And I am glad.

Prayer Reflection

Mine: It's hard to say, Lord, but I'm going to say it: "Thanks
for the severe, no option allowed, evaluation." Through
my pain you taught me a lesson I needed. Gentle me as I
evaluate others.

—Hurt, but Recovering

Yours: _____

_____

_____

The greatest among you will be your servant. For whoever exalts himself will be humbled, and whoever humbles himself will be exalted.

Matthew 23:11, 12

25 THE QUIET ONE

When S. Jay Hostetler, veteran missionary to both India and Africa, returned to the United States from a stay in Ghana, he came to the Belmont Church to speak. It was the last church he had pastored, the church I attend.

As he spoke to us that morning he mentioned things and people, relationships and contacts from Belmont, that had blessed S. Jay and his wife richly in their last stay overseas. I listened with attention. During that African mission I had written S. Jay and Ida several long and newsy letters about Belmont, about myself, about our family.

My ears strained as he said, "There was one person at Belmont who did much to keep us in touch with this home base. I want to thank that person this morning."

I thought of the letters I had sent. I did not smile. I wanted to look surprised when he mentioned the name. And I was surprised.

S. Jay said, "I am deeply appreciative to Virginia Reiff, who faithfully mailed us the church bulletins for every service. We eagerly devoured every one of them while in Ghana."

I felt the air go out of the self-image I had been inflating. Virginia, quiet and unobtrusive, had been mentioned. She was the one.

For several days the incident kept popping back into my mind. It depressed me. True, no one knew what I had been thinking—no one but God and me—yet the memory was disturbing. Then God stepped directly into the act.

He said, "Bob, what you did was fine, but you did it for the wrong reason. You wrote those letters cleverly back then, wanting to reflect a bit of glory to yourself. Virginia sent the bulletins out of love. Your motivation was different. Right?"

I mumbled, "Perhaps. It's hard to remember." Then I added in self-defense, "I think I wanted also to show Jay and Ida that I cared."

But God, psychiatrist that He is, said, "Maybe, but your thoughts back there in church just before Virginia's name was mentioned tell the story most clearly: your anticipation, your surprise, your disappointment, your depression. Those things speak volumes."

And I said softly, this time knowing my inner feelings and motivation, "You're right, Lord. And I'm sorry."

God accepted my confession. But He had more things to say before He let me run off to lick my wounds. God's last words are usually the clincher.

"Bob, your name has often appeared in the church bulletin and papers. That's where man looks. But as Samuel said, I look on the inside of a person, on the heart. Okay?"

I nodded, sadness all mixed up with happiness inside. My bruised ego healed, and I realized once more how God loves the quiet person who serves out of love, not for self-gratification.

Prayer Reflection

Mine: Father, I've done some things that others thought worthwhile. Fine, but why did I do them? Dear One, I should have done them in the name of Jesus, but instead, at times, I gloried in seeing my own by-line. I hoarded the praise instead of turning it over to You. And I had my reward. I really want to bring glory to You. Help me. Please?

—Bob

Yours: _____

_____

_____

If you remain silent at this time, relief and deliverance ... will arise from another place.... And who knows but that you have come to royal position for such a time as this?

Esther 4:14

26 HEAVENLY INTERRUPTION

I had been asked to talk to a group of grade schoolchildren at the public library during the summer months. The librarian suggested the subject of astronomy. So I brought over one of the school's telescopes, plus some other astronomical equipment, and had a delightful time talking about "Spaceship Earth" as it journeys around the sun, which in turn carries it through the heavens. We talked about the planets, keeping everything pretty low key. The audience of some two dozen, probably from first grade through sixth, were attentive, quiet, delightful. A few parents were present and a reporter from a nearby newspaper.

At the close of our looking through the telescope at some distant roof shingles, my mini-lecture nearly finished, I ventured into a simple explanation of how all this marvel of earth, solar system, and universe might have come about. Most science books mention two theories about the origin of the universe, most astronomers accepting one of them. They may accept the "Big Bang" theory which suggests that the universe of today was once in one compact mass, "exploded" outward, and is still expanding. Or, they may believe that the universe is eternal, has always been, will always be, and so identify with the "Constant State" hypothesis.

So I mentioned the two, wrote them down on my little blackboard, said a few words about them, and prepared to wind things up. Then God got in the act.

He whispered, "You could mention the 'Special Creation' idea also and bring in Me."

And I thought, "I could." But my time was long over. Would the librarian sitting on the floor with the children appreciate my bringing in the religious aspect? At school where my position is known, my status established, I bring it in, but I wondered about the importance of it here. And there's that reporter, and the listening parents. True, Madeline Murray O'Hare wasn't sitting there, but the public library seemed awfully public. Would these small children care, or remember, or be impressed with that fact amidst all the science I had showered upon them?

It's strange how one can rationalize—strange how quickly God and I were going back and forth, lickety-split in conversation. It happened in a matter of seconds. God begged just a bit, said, "I wish you wouldn't think so much, Bob, just do it. Do it for Me."

So I did. It's hard to resist God. I sketched quickly the

Genesis story and quietly added that this was the account that I accepted.

When the meeting was over, and I was disassembling the six-inch telescope in preparation for returning it to school, the reporter came over to finish gathering a bit of data. Then he said, "I'm so glad you brought in that third 'theory.' I'm a fresh Christian, born again, only a year old in the new life. What you said was affirming to me."

Wow! My heart pounded as I saw God at work again through Christ in that brother's life, through me, as I tacked on that third possibility. We talked a bit more, rejoicing in one another's belief.

Going back to school, then home, God didn't have to say a word, just listen. I kept saying, "Thank you, Lord," "Praise your name," "Sure glad I listened," "Keep right on talking," "Sorry I even questioned it."

When I notice my friend's by-line in the paper, I always read it. He's my Christian brother. If I hadn't listened to God, I might never have met him.

Prayer Reflection

Mine: I'm finding Father, that when You want me to say something, there's a reason. Like today, there was Larry Williams listening, that new one in Christ Jesus. It was perfect timing on Your part, and I almost blew it. I'm busting with joy tonight that I let You use me.

                                        —Call Me Channel Bob

Yours: _____

_____

_____

I [Jesus] am sending you out like sheep among wolves. Therefore
be as shrewd as snakes and as innocent as doves.

Matthew 10:16

27 THE FERTILIZER THAT
BACKFIRED

There's a bare spot in our backyard by the Chinese elm this
summer. And I know why.

This spring when I was fertilizing the lawn, I stopped at
that spot to fill the spreader. In the process I spilled a
quantity of fertilizer on the ground. I scooped up most of it,
spread the rest around with my fingers, and figured it was
"good enough."

It was not.

On the fertilizer bag it says, "Does not burn when used as
directed." But I had not done as directed. I had over-
fertilized. When the rains came and dissolved the fertilizer,

the grass withered and died. There are fancy words in biology to describe what happened, words like "plasmolysis," "loss of turgor," "exosmosis," and the like. But more simply put, I had "burned" the grass. Since that time, by heavy watering, I have diluted the fertilizer in that area and washed it deep below the grass roots. I know the grass will eventually grow again.

But for the present I have a good reminder. When I walk by that barren spot I think of what can happen during the process of Christian witnessing. Sometimes we "pour it on" too heavily, we "run it in the ground." We are not tactful, too "pushy," too impatient. We want things to happen too quickly, we want to prove to God and fellowmen how "good a witness" we can give. And as a result we overdose.

The bare patch of ground amidst the green grass says something to me. It says, "The sinner needs to be treated gently with the Holy Spirit measuring out both the quality and quantity of witness given. If we are too forceful, too demanding, we may delay that Spirit's work in a sinner's life."

Our witness, like mercy, should fall as the gentle rain.

Prayer Reflection

Mine: King Jesus, being Your ambassador is heavy, mighty heavy. How about a double portion of Your Spirit to ease the load?

—An Eager but Anxious Servant

Yours: _____

_____

_____

I have been very zealous for the Lord God Almighty.... I am the only one left.

1 Kings 19:10

28 THE LOVE GIFT

The letter had a Canadian postmark and carried the return address of a church in Edmonton, Alberta. As a Christian schoolteacher, who writes as an avocation and occasionally goes on a weekend speaking jaunt to some church, I open such mail with mixed feelings. A letter like that often falls into one of two categories. It can contain a complaint about something I wrote or something I said; or the letter may make a request for service—an article to write, a church that wants me to spend a weekend with them.

I was feeling sorry for myself that day with so many duties pressing in upon me. I expected the worst of the letter and let it rest unopened on the desk.

That evening before I retired, I saw the letter again and knew that I was being childish in my thoughts. I slit it open and dumped the contents on the desk. A letter and a check fell out.

Puzzled, I picked up the check. It was for no small sum. I didn't recognize the signature. Then I turned to the letter.

It was from the treasurer of a Canadian church, one where I had never been. In his church was a member who knew me and who wished to send me what he called a "love gift." And the giver wished to remain anonymous. He was giving it through the church. The check bore the name of the church and the signature of the church treasurer.

I was overwhelmed. All my miserable selfish feelings of the past few hours came rolling back in review. As I have grown older I find that the emotions I once curbed now are less easily hidden. And the tears began to flow.

I knelt beside the desk. The only thing I could pray was, "Lord, I am not worthy. I am no longer worthy to be called Your son."

Like the prodigal son, I got no further. God is so generous with His forgiveness. It came flowing in, flooding, healing.

Yet gently He said to me, "Try to live more worthy of My love, the love of others."

And I promised.

Prayer Reflection

Mine: Lord, loving one's self a bit seems okay to me, but loving one's self to the point where you fear correction or tasks from the Lord, is a bummer. It's a wicked combination of pride and selfishness. Chalk another one up against me.

—One Who Gets Stuck on Himself

Yours: _____

_____

_____

And when you stand praying, if you hold anything against anyone, forgive him, so that your Father in heaven may forgive you your sins.

Mark 11:25

29 THE CANCER CURE

His letter appeared in the "Letters to the Editor" column in one of our church papers. It was in response to an article which I had written earlier for that paper. In the letter he sharply disagreed with what I had written, and in that sharpness sliced me into small pieces.

For days that public letter was a burden to me. It was often the last thing I thought of as I retired and the first thing in the morning. I knew that it was cancerizing me.

Then God suggested a solution. I sensed Him saying to me, "Pray for Brother_____." I told God, "I can't." And God said, "You must."

Thus my burden was doubled. Thoughts of the letter were still there, and God kept reminding me that I was to pray for the brother with the sharp pen.

So I ventured out in prayer. My "enemy" was a teacher, so I prayed for his success as he taught. I prayed for his health, for his safety as he drove. Then God enlarged my thinking, my concern. I prayed for his family, for his church. I prayed that he would have wisdom in making choices, in his relationships in the town where he lived. The Lord was faithful in His promise to teach me how to pray for this brother.

And, of course, it happened. The weight of the critical letter disappeared. It still popped into my mind upon occasion, and when it did I thanked God for the stepping-stone it provided. I leaped from it into prayer for the man that I had now come to love.

Surely our God is a Worker of miracles, a Converter of men. He took a burden and changed it into a blessing. God reached out and touched me, and my adversary became my friend. It was not he who needed to be changed; it was I.

Prayer Reflection

Mine: You know, I'm pretty proud, Lord. And upon occasion (in fact, upon lots of occasions), I'm not very nonresistant. Yet I know loving sure beats hating. Thanks so much for helping me to win this one.

—Still Learning

Yours: _____

_____

_____

But you, O Lord, are a compassionate and gracious God, slow to anger, abounding in love and faithfulness.

Psalm 86:15

30 PATIENCE UNLIMITED

The rusted wire-cutting pliers I found were so badly corroded that they no longer functioned. The jaws were locked in a half-open position. I squeezed the handles with all my strength, but they budged not a millimeter. By the manufacturer's mark upon them, I could tell that they were once a fine piece of equipment.

I was about to discard them when I thought of the penetrating oil I had in the garage, a liquid that was highly advertised as being successful at freeing up rusted, "frozen" parts. I decided to give it a go.

Carefully I squirted the solution along the rust-lined

crevices, joints that had once been free to move. I gently tapped with a hammer on the rigid grips. Nothing happened. The pliers remained unmovable.

I continued my efforts for fifteen minutes, then a half an hour. There were no visible results. But I hated to give up. I had an investment in the pliers—my time, my hopes.

Finally I sensed a brief giving, a tiny movement. I applied more lubricant, more tender tapping. Now, rapidly the pliers yielded, eventually moving freely.

Today the pliers are in my toolbox, a precious reminder of God's love, the lubricant that frees us, that enables us as Christians to move for Him. How patiently God works with us, continually applying that love, His Holy Spirit gently tapping and striving with us! Finally we respond to that love, we move at the Spirit's leading, we are set free to be used in kingdom service. God's labor of love with us is a beautiful thing.

Prayer Reflection

Mine: We talk about the patience of Job, but we really ought to talk about the patience of God. Father, thanks for having worked with some mighty stubborn, bullheaded, mule-like people, including me.

—Among the Top Ten

Yours: _____

_____

_____

The heavens declare the glory of God; the skies proclaim the work of his hands. Day after day they pour forth speech; night after night they display knowledge.

Psalm 19:1, 2

31 COMMENTS FROM THE COMETS

It's thrilling how God can take a secular event and allow the Christian special insight so that he may draw from it a spiritual application to bless his soul.

Recently while watching a film on comets in my science class, I heard the commentator say, "Comets shine only by reflected light.... The closer they come to the sun, the more brilliant they shine.... Comets are dying things, for each time the comet makes its circuit around the sun, it loses some of its material and goes away a little smaller than it came...."

I appreciated the scientific facts of the film, but I appreciated even more what the Holy Spirit laid on my heart as the scientific truths were translated into spiritual truths: "As a Christian, I shine only when I reflect Christ. . . . The closer I come to Him, the more brilliant that reflection of Him will be. . . . As a Christian, I should be dying to myself, decreasing as He increases, the ego in me becoming smaller every time I circle around His glory."

But when the film came to a close with its sad prediction of the eventual death of the comet, there the parallel ended. I remembered Daniel 12:3, and I knew that one day I too would "shine like the brightness of the heavens . . . like the stars for ever and ever."

In the quiet dark schoolroom, just before the lights were turned on, I breathed a prayer of thanks to God for the lesson He taught me as a Christian while I looked at the life of a comet.

Prayer Reflection

Mine: I just praise You for Your creation. You speak to me through what You made. Every star twinkles out its separate 'I love you,' a valentine from You.
— Feeling Loved and Liking It

Yours: _____

_____

_____

Wealth is worthless in the day of wrath, but righteousness delivers from death.

Proverbs 11:4

32 LIGHTNING LESSON

Late one night during a terrific thunder and lightning storm we heard an earsplitting crack that brought our daughter flying down the stairs in alarm. It seemed close.

The next morning we found out how close. The trunk of the tall poplar beside the garage was split, the bark hanging in shreds, pieces of wood scattered over the yard.

As I viewed the damage, my first thought was, "It's going to cost me at least $150 to get a tree trimmer out here to clean up this mess."

That week a stranger came to see me. We stood there in the driveway talking and he noticed the split trunk, the hanging bark. Casually he asked, "Lightning?"

I nodded glumly. "Right."

He looked from the shattered tree to the house sixty feet away, his eyes traveling up the cedar shake siding to the window just below the gable. It was the window of my daughter's room.

He let out a long whistle, then said in gamblers' terms, "That was almost on the money, wasn't it?"

His comment rocked me back. The lightning bolt missed our home, my daughter, my wife, myself. Yet I considered myself a loser, out $150.

I realized how wrong my priorities had been. Dollar signs caused me to miss how God had so mercifully spared us.

I looked at the tree again and said to myself, "Forgive me, Lord. The tree loss and expense I can easily stand. People are not so readily replaced. Thank you for showing me through the words of a gambler how gracious You really are."

Prayer Reflection

Mine: You know my weaknesses so well, Father. This depression boy is scared to death that someday he might be broke, penniless. And yet I've confessed You as Lord, my Provider and Sustainer. Somehow, it doesn't quite fit together.

—Still Not Perfect

Yours: _____

_____

_____

Other seed fell among thorns, which grew up and choked the plants.

Matthew 13:7

33 LIFE IN THE CEMETERY

For the past ten years our family has cared for a little country cemetery. We found the abandoned half-acre burial spot just a few miles from our home, the last resting place of my great-great-grandparents.

When we discovered that cemetery it was filled with wild blackberry bushes, small walnut trees, weeds, and tangled vines. It was ugly, no beauty about it. Not even dandelions could grow under that thick cover.

That first summer we cleared the wild growth away and began the weekly mowing of the cemetery. Grass, long hidden from the sun, began to flourish.

Several years after the original clearing daffodils and grape hyacinths appeared. Then came the lilies of the valley, followed by iris. Peonies next announced themselves by lovely flowering. Now roses have struggled into bloom in two different areas of the cemetery.

I stood there the other day and marveled at what had happened. The flowering potential had been there the first time we saw that weed-filled cemetery. But there had been no chance for the flowers to bloom.

Yet I marveled even more as I thought of how it is in our own lives. The kind deeds, the loving thoughts, the tender ministering of others have no chance to grow when sin flourishes, chokes, and consumes us. But once we remove the evil from our lives, then the gracious plantings by loving hands in the past have an opportunity to bloom and beautify.

I stood there in the cemetery among the dead and realized once again that if the fruit of the Spirit were to live and flourish in my life for God's glory, then the "wild blackberry bushes" must be uprooted from that life. I promised Him that I would pull such selfish weeds so that His presence might be seen in me.

Prayer Reflection

Mine: It's been five years, Lord, since I made that weed-pulling promise. And I still find some "blackberry bushes" sprouting. Hit me again, Father, with Your convicting power.

—Still Struggling

Yours: _____

_____

_____

Why do you entertain evil thoughts in your hearts?

Matthew 9:4

34 THE DISAPPEARING COINS

For approximately nine weeks of the school term the small dish of pennies, nickels, and a few dimes sat on my desk in our junior high school. It was a change dish, part of an honor system for my ninth-grade science students.

It sat beside a package of graph paper. When a pupil needed a piece of paper to graph the results of an experiment we had performed, he helped himself and made his own change. It was a nonprofit system, a service to the pupils. If you had no money with you, you took a sheet, and paid later—if you remembered. No one kept records. I paid little attention to it, occasionally removing some of the larger coins and replacing the graph paper.

One morning I entered the room and the dish was empty. The morning before it had been nearly full. A student had taken the entire contents of the dish, perhaps fifty cents.

As I stood there, I boiled inside. It wasn't the amount of money stolen that irritated me. It was that I had trusted them, and someone in one of those six classes had taken my kindness and replaced it with his greed. It was an unfair exchange.

I began formulating my lecture. I would give it to each of the six classes—150 students in all. I would have plenty of bitter, sarcastic words. The person who took the money would feel my righteous indignation.

Then I thought of the 149 other students who daily saw the money, were never tempted, or resisted the temptation to take the money. And I changed my speech.

That day I told each class about what had happened. But I told each class also how proud I was of them. They knew right from wrong, and well over 99 percent practiced what they believed. How good that I could trust that high majority! I thanked them for their honesty.

I learned my lesson. For every person who does wrong, there may be a hundred who will do no wrong. The world is a much more pleasant place in which to live if we can see the good in the many instead of the evil in a few.

Prayer Reflection

Mine: Great Physician, healing Jesus, You know my specialty, but it's not a skill; it's a sickness. I'm excellent at nitpicking. I can spot a sin a mile off, but miss the good next to my nose. Have You got a pill I can take to get rid of this condemning headache of mine?

—Slightly Sick

Yours: _____

_____

_____

He [God] causes the sun to rise on the evil and the good, and sends rain on the righteous and the unrighteous.

Matthew 5:45

35 LIVING WITH THE SOUR NOTES

Our daughter, accompanist for her high school choir, came home after a concert greatly distressed over an error she had made. Her piano playing seemed flawless until her final note of one particular number. Then even my untrained ear could hear the discord.

My wife and I tried to soothe her, but she would not be comforted at the moment. The whole evening had been ruined because of that one error.

I thought later of how we magnify one mistake. My daughter forgot all the lovely notes that she had played that evening. I doubt if her single error represented one thousandth of the contribution she had made, yet she was inconsolable at the time.

I thought of how God at times allows a sour note to sound in our lives. Everything is going beautifully, then a spot of unhappiness drips into the events of the week. When it appears, like a sponge, it seems to absorb all the loveliness with which it had been surrounded.

Longfellow wrote, "Into each life some rain must fall." Yet sometimes as Christians we seem to feel that God should hold an umbrella over us continually, that every day should be a mountaintop experience.

It's not so. God builds no wall around us. How beautiful to know that not a single discordant note enters our lives except it be within His permissive will! Then on each side of that disharmony He places a beautiful symphony for us to enjoy. We should be reveling in the beauty of the past orchestration and anticipating God's next masterpiece, not majoring in the division markers God allows to be spaced between them.

To concentrate on the inharmonious notes that sound upon occasion in each of our lives is like trying to make sense out of a meaningful story by reading only the periods.

As Christians we should know better.

Prayer Reflection

Mine: Sweet Jesus, am I the world's leading complainer? Don't answer that! When a pebble of trouble falls into and ripples my sea of blessings, I guess I act like a two-year-old. I wonder that You can stand me, but thanks for doing so.
—Mark Me Grateful

Yours: _____

_____

_____

For the foolishness of God is wiser than man's wisdom, and the weakness of God is stronger than man's strength.

1 Corinthians 1:25

36 FOLLOWING GOD'S PROGRAM

It was the closing night of the church conference, the last time I was scheduled to speak. I knew my topic. It was on the printed program, a subject for which I had carefully prepared, and my notes were at hand. But for much of that last conference day it seemed that God had been directing my thoughts to another subject.

That evening I struggled for twenty-five minutes, attempting to speak on the subject assigned. Finally I gave up. I snapped my notes shut, briefly stated my dilemma, and spoke for ten minutes on an entirely different subject centering on the point that God makes no mistakes.

I'm certain that many people present thought that I was making a mistake. I sat down frustrated, feeling that I had made a fool of myself. I blamed God for it. God reminded me that I had often made a fool of myself without His help. But that was cold comfort.

The program continued as the moderator glossed over my apparent confusion.

After the meeting I began to understand the reason why I needed to tack on the ten-minute trailer to my topic. Two weeping women, both in their early twenties, came up to tell me that my closing comments were for them. Both had been doubting God. The one quickly left without further explanation. The other stayed to tell me of the tragedy in her life, how she had lost her husband shortly after their marriage. She had been blaming God. But I had said that God made no mistakes. Through her tears she said that she was now willing to accept her husband's death.

The final affirmation came in two weeks. I received a letter from the area where I had spoken. A mother wrote to explain what happened just a few hours before I gave my final talk in her church. While feeding the chickens on their farm, she reminded God once more of a mistake He had made in the life of their family. Several years ago their eleven-year-old daughter had been killed in a tractor accident. She came to church that evening to hear me say that God made no mistakes. In her letter she explained that she would believe what I had said.

I tremble to think how close I came to failing God and those three people. I had wanted the praise of men so badly that I had nearly cost those needy ones what God wanted to share through me.

I told the Lord that He now had full rights to make a fool out of me anytime He chose. He suggested that it would be necessary again, perhaps frequently.

I am perfectly satisfied with the arrangement. After all, God makes no mistakes.

Prayer Reflection

Mine: Gracious Spirit, when I think about this particular incident in my life, I often cry. Thanks for giving me no rest that particular Sunday until I spoke on Your subject. I'll be a fool for You any day of the week.

—Simple Me

Yours: _____

_____

_____

For you know that it was not with perishable things such as silver or gold that you were redeemed from the empty way of life ... but with the precious blood of Christ, a lamb without blemish or defect.

1 Peter 1:18, 19

37 CHAMPION BLOOD DONOR

There are 24 entries on the little yellow cards I carry in my wallet. Sixteen of the entries are the names of people—A. R. Miller is 1957 was the first, while William Constant in 1980 is the last. Four are simply marked "donation."

For some time I have been a blood donor at our local hospital. I like to look at the list, recall the dear friends for whom I have specifically replaced blood. Three of those listed are now deceased. I really have enjoyed giving the blood. There is sort of a bond between myself and people on the list. I'm not sure if they experience the bond, but I do. So at times I take out that list, look at it, pray for the people still living, and rejoice that I had a chance to share with them.

Sometimes at home I innocently ask family members, "Have I recently shown you my blood bank cards?"

But before I can remove them from my wallet, they all groan and declare, "Yes, yes, you've shown them many many times." And we all laugh.

I confess I have been a wee bit proud of the list, the gallon pin my hospital gave me, the certificate marking my joining the "Gallon Donor Club."

But now, even in jest, I seldom mention it to others. God squelched me the other day.

I had been looking at the cards, reviewing the names on them, and thinking some good thoughts about them. Each card contains six entries and I have four cards, completely filled.

God said, "Bob, I'm glad you donated blood. I think it's nice. Keep it up. A Friend of yours and Mine gave blood. I guess He could carry cards like you, listing all those for whom He gave. But it would be a pretty bulky stack. You know, of course, He's got you beat all to pieces."

I knew there was something coming that I needed, and I got ready for God's punch line. It came quickly as He said, "Our mutual Friend is My Son Jesus Christ."

It hit me like a ton of bricks. How right, how right! He donated His blood. The entire world of then, of now, and the world to come was on His list: "In him we have redemption through his blood, the forgiveness of sins, in accordance with the riches of God's grace that he lavished on us" (Ephesians 1:7).

I thought: "I gave a pint at a time, but Jesus Christ gave it all. In a few weeks my body has replaced the blood I gave. The actual giving takes perhaps 30 minutes. Jesus bled for hours from the crown of thorns alone. Then for three hours

He bled from hands and feet. And finally from His side.

I lay in luxury on a custom-made couch at the blood bank room as I gave my blood. Jesus hung in disgrace and agony on a cross when He gave His.

People who were credited for my pint of blood wrote me, called me, expressed their thanks profusely. Jesus was cursed when He gave His. They gave me orange juice after I donated. Jesus was given sour wine.

As I made the comparisons, my four yellow cards recording 24 donations paled into insignificance.

I've heard many ministers in sermons and prayers speak about the precious blood of Jesus. I guess I've talked about it also. They are glib words, easily spoken. Did I really mean them? I cannot say.

But now I know something for sure. I'll never give again, never pull those yellow cards from my wallet, without a silent or audible, "Thank you, Jesus, for donating Your blood to me."

Now I'll mean it.

Prayer Reflection

Mine: What did the song say? Something about counting your richest gain as loss and pouring contempt on all your pride? That's me, Lord. I helped 24 people at no cost to myself. Your Son helped the world at unmeasurable cost to You and Him. What can I say?

—Color Me Ashamed

Yours: _____

_____

_____

Be on your guard; stand firm in the faith; be men of courage; be strong.

1 Corinthians 16:13

38 GOD LEFT IT UP TO ME

I was attending Indiana University summer school at Bloomington, Indiana, when God gave me a test that I nearly flunked. We both knew what the right answer was, but I didn't want to put it down. I wanted to fudge a bit, try a substitute answer, and still expect full credit from God. I hardly thought it fair of Him to lead me on and then throw a monkey wrench into the machinery.

I had the family with me on campus and as usual our funds were limited. I knew that I would need a part-time job to help subsidize the summer study. My wife was busy with two small children. So I applied at student services for a job that would allow me to put in 15-20 hours per week. It would enable us to survive.

Along with several others I was sent to the library where I found what seemed to be the ideal answer. They were in need of part-time library assistants to hand out reserved books and sort out returning ones. It would help me to earn money, and I could do some studying on the job when not busy.

Standing with the others, listening to the librarian's instructions, I smiled my acceptance. Then the librarian tossed in the bombshell that upset my little apple cart. She said, "And you'll need to rotate for the Sunday schedule, perhaps working every other Sunday."

My heart sank. We had already committed ourselves to attending the little Mennonite Church at Bean Blossom. Sunday work conflicted with my convictions. I looked quickly for a way out, a way to hang onto the job almost within my grasp. Excuses flew rapidly through my head.

This library work was a service task. The library needed to stay open on Sunday for some. And there was the money. It was not every Sunday. "Lord, wouldn't You allow it?"

And God said, "Bob, it's your decision." And He moved off to the side of the room and left me there on my own.

The librarian looked around the half circle of needy students, waiting for our nods of acceptance.

There were no protests. It seemed agreeable.

I sighed reluctantly and said, "I'm sorry, but I can't work on Sunday. I have other commitments." It wasn't a very outspoken testimony, about one-half horsepower, and said little about my convictions. But it was the best I could do for the moment.

The librarian said, "Well, I'm sorry, but the Sunday work goes with the position."

I turned to leave. I didn't feel good about the decision to speak up, even though I knew it was right. I felt like money was being taken from me that I needed. I tossed God a dirty look and said, "You may see the righteous begging bread *this* summer."

Then another of the applicants spoke up. She said, "Sunday work would really work out best for me." She gave her reasons, then said, "I would be happy to get in as much Sunday work as I can. Perhaps I could take this man's Sunday shift and he could take some of my weekday hours."

My heart rose a notch. I looked at the librarian. She nodded. "I believe that would work out. Let's see how the schedule will look."

That's how the summer went, beautiful. It worked out perfect for us.

Then I knew why God moved aside that day of the job interview. He knew how it could end, but He wanted me to make the decision with no pressure from Him.

I'm stronger because He didn't frost the cake ahead of time for me. He didn't tell me the happy ending of the story before I went to the trouble of reading the book.

God doesn't dangle us like puppets suspended from strings, causing us to dance at His directions, smoothing the way to perfection before us. He gives us some hills to climb.

And I am glad.

Prayer Reflection

Mine: When You put me on my own, so often I goof it up. But when I don't, I feel ten feet tall. Thanks for the chance to grow.

> —One Who Needs Every Chance
> He Can Get

Yours: _____

_____

_____

"Here is a boy with five small barley loaves and two small fish, but how far will they go among so many?" ... Jesus then took the loaves, gave thanks and distributed to those who were seated as much as they wanted.... When they all had enough to eat ... they gathered them and filled twelve baskets ... left over.

John 6:9-13

39 THE LITTLE THING

My wife accepted the telephone call for me. A retired schoolteacher was in the hospital and would like to see me. Could I possibly stop in?

And I did.

There I found Nelly. It was her second operation, with not the greatest prognosis ahead. She and her husband, both Christians, were looking for a miracle. That's what was needed. I stayed briefly, had prayer with them, kissed Nelly on the cheek, and left.

But she stayed in my mind. That night I called her husband and asked him if there was anything I could do.

"No," he replied, "we just want to thank you so much for coming to the hospital. Both Nelly and I deeply appreciated it."

"It was such a little thing," I murmured. "I was at the hospital anyway to visit my sister."

Then God spoke through Don. Over the telephone a beautiful statement and a bit of correction, a word of wisdom I needed. Nelly's husband said, "Oh, but the little things come much easier, and they add up."

So often I want to do the spectacular. I want to move the mountains, to cast them into the sea. I want to feed the five thousand, to heal the lame man, to open the eyes of the blind. I want to speak to the Pilates of the world, to correct the Pharisees. I want to cast out devils, to sense that they are subject to me. I want to preach like Billy Graham.

Why? I think I have good reasons. There are such great needs in the world. I am bothered by them. I wish I could solve the refugee problems in the Middle East, the Far East. I would like to have the answer to malnutrition in Africa, in South America. I would house the migrant worker, provide loving care for the aged.

I would write the great American novel, one that would speak to the world, restore morality to this nation, turn us back to God.

I have done none of these things. Nor is it likely that I shall. Limited abilities, advancing age, suggest not.

But Don Smith said the little things count. He said they added up. He should know. He and Nelly have not yet received the miracle they seek. But they are rejoicing in the visit of friends, in the cards, the telephone calls, the little miracles of caring and love.

I called Don to assure him, and was assured myself. I belittled my contribution and was gently reproved. Through my brother God spoke to me. I have been learning not to despise the day of small things (Zechariah 4:10).

Sometimes it is only the handshake I give. But I try to do it with intensity, with concentration. Sometimes it is only a touch on the arm or the shoulder, but in that contact I want to say, "I'm with you in your need."

Or it's patient listening when my brother calls and pours out his heart to me about his family problems. I do nothing except listen, but by it I say, "You need to talk, to empty yourself, so pour out your troubles to me."

I can't afford to send a dozen long-stemmed roses, but I've learned to ask for a single one at the florists and to deliver it with a thirty-dollar smile.

If I waited until I could send the hundred-dollar check, the costly bouquet, until the novel was written, I might contribute nothing.

I'm learning to be content with giving bits of myself, small loaves, little fishes. God is blessing, multiplying them, with many fragments left over for new distribution.

Prayer Reflection

Mine: Lord, forgive me for wanting to make the big splash, to excite the "Ohs" and "Ahs" of others. Lay on me every single day a little load to lift, a smile to hand out for free. I don't have to set the world on fire, but let me warm up someone for You.

—One of Your Little Ones

Yours: _____

_____

_____

You, dear children, are from God and have overcome them, because the one who is in you is greater than the one who is in the world.

1 John 4:4

40 FLYING STANDBY FOR THE LORD

When we landed half an hour late at O'Hare International Airport in Chicago, I ran quickly to the gate down the hall for my connecting flight to Bismarck, North Dakota. The waiting room was empty except for the airline attendant who was taking down the Bismarck destination sign from behind the checking counter. I gasped, looked out the wide windows, and saw my plane taxiing out to a main runway. What I feared was confirmed. I had missed my flight.

Later that day, after many telephone calls and much discussion with ticket agents, I had a questionable standby reservation that might get me to Minot, North Dakota, perhaps eventually to Glendive, Montana, where I wanted to go. By this time the man who had driven three hours from Glendive to Bismarck to pick me up would be driving back to Montana alone, his trip fruitless. Even if I got out of O'Hare, I could still be bumped from the plane at Minneapolis or Grand Forks by someone with a confirmed reservation. The whole thing was a mess. I felt like crying.

As I waited the long hours for my possible flight, I talked with God. I reviewed the experience thus far. I had been asked to serve at a youth rally this weekend nearly a year ago. I had suggested they get someone else. But they came back and begged. The result? I had yielded. Now this. So I said, "Lord, it sort of looks like I was right the first time about coming. I should have stuck to my guns. I feel like calling it quits and heading back to Elkhart."

As I sat there in the world's busiest airport terminal building, the answer came quick and sharp in the form of a question: "Are you any better than Daniel?" And I knew immediately what Scripture the Lord had in mind.

I pulled my Bible out of my briefcase and flipped to Daniel 10. I read how an angel came to Daniel and said, "Do not be afraid, Daniel. Since the first day that you set your mind to gain understanding ... your words were heard, and I have come in response to them. But the prince of the Persian kingdom resisted me twenty-one days. Then Michael ... came to help me ... now I have come to explain to you what will happen. . . . "

Then I began to understand. Satan did not want me in Montana. He was fighting God's plans, delaying me, even as Satan resisted God answering Daniel's prayers. But God was on my side and the fur was flying as the two forces fought. Should I throw in the towel when God was in my corner?

The fear of not getting on the plane tonight, of finding

myself stranded in Minneapolis or Grand Forks began to drift away. If God was on my side, how could I lose?

I was feeling that God really wanted me at Glendive, that He was greater than Satan's delaying tactics. I knew that God was going all out for me, that I would need to do the same for Him and pull out all the stops.

God said, "When I want you someplace, Bob, I'll get you there." Then he added, with a bit of humor, "I'll get you there, if you'll just stand by."

So there at O'Hare, in front of North Central Airline's counter, I curled my thumb and first finger into that familiar okay sign and said, "Gotcha, Lord. Thanks a million."

And God answered, "No trouble on this end."

When I got to Minot, North Dakota, unbumped at any intermediary stop, I found the Roy Martins waiting for me to take me on the next leg of my journey. I was so happy to see them that I kissed them both.

Once more it was confirmed to me what some Christians have never doubted: When God is on your side, you're a winner. God may have to send you by second-class, but every letter He mails gets there. What a Postmaster!

Prayer Reflection

Mine: Father, when I look at where I've been, seen your loving arms lifting me up, I get the goose bumps! I can't get over it! You've got an answer for everything. Thanks for being in my corner that special weekend.

—Grateful Me

Yours: _____

_____

Each tree is recognized by its own fruit. People do not pick figs from thornbushes, or grapes from briers. The good man brings forth good things out of the good stored up in his heart, and the evil man brings evil things out of the evil stored up in his heart. For out of the overflow of his heart his mouth speaks.

Luke 6:44, 45

41 THE AFFIRMATION

I teach in a large integrated junior high school in northern Indiana. For some thirty years I have taught children in grades seven, eight, and nine. It has not always been easy, but it has its moments of priceless joy. And during that time I have learned that some of the more significant teacher-student exchanges take place in the halls, not the classrooms.

I sensed this the other week when a cute little seventh-grade black girl stopped me in the hall and said, "Mr. Baker, you're a Christian, aren't you?"

I returned her smile with one of my own, pleased with her observation, but wondering how she knew it. I didn't have her in class, and we had never exchanged a word to my knowledge. So I said, "Yes, I'm a Christian, but how did you know?"

She answered with great simplicity of judgment, "Because I know some kids in your classes, and they say you never cuss or holler at them."

Then she gave me a happy wave of her hand, and scurried down the hall to join her waiting friends.

She made my day.

Prayer Reflection

Mine: This week, Lord, I want to affirm someone in their Christian life. Let me know who it's to be. I'll be waiting.

Love,
Bob

Yours: _____

_____

_____

For he will command his angels concerning you to guard you in all your ways; they will lift you up in their hands.

Psalm 91:11, 12a

42 MIRACLE ON ROUTE 33

When I hear Christians use the word "lucky" in referring to themselves, I shudder. I think God does too. We've talked about it, He and I, and He knows I'm trying to eliminate it from my vocabulary. I keep finding proof that the word isn't valid in my life. The last incident happened several winters ago halfway between Elkhart and Fort Wayne, Indiana, on U.S. Highway 33.

Wife, Anna Mae, and I were on our way to Fort Wayne Mennonite Church, where I was speaking at the invitation of the Dennis Roth family.

The highway was clear in spots, icy in others, so we drove

at a modest speed. Cars seemed to travel in clumps that morning, approaching us in twos and threes with spaces between. We watched them with care.

As I drove, the right front wheel dropped off the edge of the highway to the berm, followed by the rear. The drop was extremely slight, perhaps half an inch, hardly discernible. I anticipated no trouble as I turned to the left to regain the highway. But there was trouble.

The car went into a slide and I fought frantically to bring it under control. Nothing helped. The steering wheel was useless. For some 200 yards, perhaps more, we moved terrifyingly down the highway from one side to the other. Trees and telephone poles tore by us in rapid succession.

I could think of only one thing as I tried helplessly to bring the car out of its skid. I thought of my wife beside me. I realized that because of my carelessness we were going to have an accident, that it would bring her injury, perhaps death. It was not a flashback, but a flash-ahead. I saw the ambulance, the hospital room. I found myself saying aloud, "Anna Mae, I'm sorry."

Then the car fishtailed completely around, and I looked despairingly back up the road from which we had come, awaiting the impact of another car or a tree. Instead the car slammed into a high snowbank located at that particular spot beside the highway. We were blinded by a shower of snow thrown up as snow and car met. Everything came to a sudden stop. The motor stalled. Silence reigned.

For a moment we sat there. Trembling, I tried the engine. It started. A wide-eyed motorist pulled up beside us and looked questioningly across at us. I waved him on. I pulled cautiously to the right side of the road and off the highway. There seemed to be no damage and we took time for a prayer of thanksgiving.

When we told our experience at the Roths, our hosts for the day, they shared how they had prayed for us that morning, asking God to spare us from danger, to give us safety. Things began to fall into place.

Just outside Goshen that morning, a few miles from home, we saw a hitchhiker. By myself, I sometimes pick up such a person if he looks "safe." But if my wife or daughter is along, I'm reluctant to pick them up. This hitchhiker did not appeal to me. Yet I felt a strange urge to pick him up, questioned my wife, and she left it up to me. It would delay us, but it was all right with her.

We picked up the thumber, delivered him to his destination, losing only a few minutes in the process.

But it placed us in a different time slot when we hit that icy spot and slid down the highway. It placed us between clumps of traffic approaching from the opposite direction, traffic we could easily have crashed into had we arrived a few minutes earlier, if we had been in a slightly different sequence of time. Contrary to our usual procedure we picked up the hitchhiker, delayed ourselves a bit, fell into that open stretch of highway when we had no control over our car. Down the road God had seen what was to happen, and prayer-pressured by those in Fort Wayne, He delayed us and preserved us.

Did it really happen that way? Was it divinely planned? Or did we "luck out" and by chance find ourselves at the right spot at the right time?

You may describe it as being "lucky" if you care to. Not me. I believe God intervened. Sixty miles away from the family who prayed, we "had" to pick up the hitchhiker. We were delayed and slotted into the empty highway spot when we had no control over our car, coming miraculously to a safe stop.

"Lord" and "luck" are both four-letter words. I sense that the Lord, not luck, is in control of my life. I'm not a bit of flotsam, a chip of wood, tossed helplessly and hopelessly where the tides of luck hurl me.

I praise God that He cares, hears His children's call, touches my life, yea, even holds it in the hollow of His hand.

Prayer Reflection

Mine: Father above, Father all around me, Father within me, You are not the "luck" of my life but the Lord of my life. I really want and pray for Your daily interference. I do best when You are in charge.

—Your Thankful Highway Slider

Yours: _____

_____

_____

Now we see but a poor reflection; then we shall see face to face. Now I know in part; then I shall know fully, even as I am fully known.

1 Corinthians 13:12

43 SEEING YOURSELF

Some of my closest moments with God have been as He ministered to me in a corrective manner. They are not always the most pleasant moments, yet they are the times when God is at my elbow, when I sense His gentle, yet commanding presence. He always deals with me in love.

Recently one of the members of our congregation lost his position with a local company. His release came as a shock, at an unfortunate time, just before the year-end holidays. There was some severance pay, but he had a young family, and they were in the process of purchasing a number of basics that many of us more established families already possessed. Unless he found new employment soon, things could become difficult.

Our family discussed how we might help them. Since our checking account carried a balance beyond our immediate needs, we sent them a check, suggesting they keep it as a reserve, sort of a cushion, until they saw how things worked out. It could be spent or returned. They were able to accept this offer and both our families felt happy over the arrangement.

In less than a week I received through the mail a totally unexpected gift of money from a church in Canada where I had ministered. A local store had a sales-promotion effort that netted us an extra $40 discount on a set of tires that we needed. We received another financial surprise on a second purchase when I was given a trade-in allowance that far exceeded our fondest hopes. The Lord seemed to be refunding with great promptness the money we loaned to our Christian brother.

As I thought about it while in town one morning, adding up in my mind what we had almost miraculously received and subtracting it from what we had loaned, I realized that there was only $20 difference. God's arithmetic, His prompt refunding, was marvelous.

That morning I thought to myself, "I wonder if God doesn't have another check at home in the mailbox for us covering that remaining $20?" The conviction grew on me that He did. It was as if I had already opened the envelope and the check was lying in front of me.

I hurried home that day and picked up the mail. There were no letters, only magazines and advertisements. I felt disappointed, as if God had really let me down, not honoring the faith I had in Him.

Then came that gentle, corrective moment.

God said to me, "Bob, I returned to you almost all of the money you loaned to your brother. Do you think that you could take care of the remaining $20?"

I felt deeply ashamed. Christmas was just a few weeks away. At that first Christmas God gave His all, His Son. He had received back so little from me for that supreme gift of His. Now in this present matter He had already repaid 90 percent of the investment I had made. I was dunning Him for the last payment. What sort of Christmas spirit did I have?

God made His point so well. He let me see myself. Shame leads to confession. Confession brings forgiveness. Forgiveness results in happiness.

Sometimes the best present a Christian can receive from God is a mirror.

Prayer Reflection

Mine: Lord, I don't always like what I see in myself. Sometimes I suspect I do things for the loaves and fishes You provide. I would like to serve You out of love, just because You are You, not because I am I. You didn't charge for salvation, so how come I expect triple pay for a little overtime?

—El Cheapo

Yours: _____

_____

_____

Wait for the Lord; be strong and take heart and wait for the Lord.
Psalm 27:14

44 THE GENTLE KNOCK

Sometimes in teaching one becomes discouraged. It's not all peaches and cream—three months of vacation every year and children rising up to call you blessed.

In over thirty years of teaching I've had my highs and lows. There are times at the end of the day when you wonder if it's worth it—the educational preparation, the hassle with administrators, with parents, with students.

Then God reminds me of Jim. And as I remember, I smile.

Jim was a pistol in class—hard and cruel, clever and devious. We had conflict after conflict. Perhaps some of it was my fault, but not all of it was. Finally came the showdown.

As I talked with Jim's father, it became a question of whether the father would believe me or his son. The latest incident had been serious—a prank in the lab that endangered others. I had plenty of evidence that pointed to Jim. I was nearly 100 percent sure, but Jim denied his guilt and maintained innocence. The father believed his son. So I backed down and changed the conduct grade.

Later I talked with the young man after school. I looked into his hard face and said, "Jim, if you ever decide that I was right and that you were wrong, come back and tell me. It would be good for you and good for me."

His face was immobile and unexpressive as he left my office. I felt only contempt from him. We maintained an armed truce for the remainder of the year.

Jim went on to high school and I saw little of him. He played high school athletics and I read about him in the paper. He came back to our junior high school to see some of our basketball games. Each time I saw him, I spoke to him. Each time he ignored me. I gritted my teeth.

Later Jim went to college. During his Christmas break he came over to our school, which was still in session, to visit his favorite teachers. I saw him down the hall, but I knew he hadn't come to visit me. I simply waved and entered my office, not pausing to see if he waved in return. I confess it was painful to see him. The old memories were resurrected.

Later that day there was a gentle knock at the office door. It was Jim.

He stepped inside the office at my invitation. Without a bit of hesitation, he said with a smile, "Mr. Baker, you were right." We both knew what he was talking about.

I could have hugged him; perhaps I should have.

We talked a bit. When he left I knew that everything in the past thirty years of teaching was worthwhile.

Now when my cross seems a bit heavy, when the gray days come three or four in a row, when it seems that everything is going down the drain with some pupil, when I've lost a battle in which I'm sure I'm right, then God says, "Remember Jim."

For some the rallying cry is, "Remember the Alamo." For me it's, "Remember Jim." I see him at my door, rejoice at his smile, and hear him say, "Mr. Baker, you were right."

I think God puts a "Jim" in every life. It may be a person or an incident, but there comes the day when He blows the clouds away, when the rainbow appears.

I love to feed on such memories as the one I have shared. I can't recall all the incidents in the classroom where Jim gave me a bad time, the nights I lay awake in bed and wondered what to do with him.

But I'll never forget his gentle knock, his smile, the words that said to me, "I'm sorry."

With such a flag waving in front of me, I should be good for another thirty years—more or less.

Prayer Reflection

Mine: Chief Accountant, I'm wrong so often that it's tough to be right and miss the credit. When the "Jims" don't come back, let me remember that you keep the final records and will balance the books for the last time. I worry too much, don't I, Lord?

                                                            —The Worrier

Yours: _____

_____

_____

When Solomon finished praying, fire came down from heaven and consumed the burnt offering and the sacrifices, and the glory of the Lord filled the temple.... When all the Israelites saw the fire coming down, and the glory of the Lord above the temple, they knelt on the pavement with their faces to the ground and they worshiped and gave thanks to the Lord.

2 Chronicles 7:1, 3a

45 APPLAUDING GOD

In our church on Sunday morning we have a time called "Concerns of the Church." You can stand, call attention to a need, give a word of affirmation, offer a personal testimony.

One Sunday morning a stranger stood in our church service and spoke of her epileptic child. She told of the seizures that came in spite of medication.

Then her voice breaking, tears flowing, she told how that some friends had special prayer for her afflicted child this past week. Since that time the daily seizures had not appeared. She stood there in our church and thanked God for healing her child. Then she sat down.

The church was quiet. In that emotionally packed moment, captivated and caught up by the woman's faith, her answered prayer, I thought of what happens when we attend an athletic event and a spectacular play is made. Then we applaud. And I thought, "We should clap now for this woman's faith, the prayers that were made, God's answer."

But I remembered that it was church. And I was quiet. And so was everyone else.

Later that day I thought of the impressive moment of the morning, when we listened in wonderment.

But the Father up above we ignored. I excused myself for my quietness. I said, "Lord, Your house is a house of prayer, not a place for loud noises, tumult, applause."

God said, "True, but prayer is supplication, worship, adoration, praise. A woman prayed in faith and a child was healed. Was that not a call to praise, to worship?"

My mind is made up. When it happens again, when God is so honored in our church, and He will be, then I shall clap my hands in applause to Him. Let others look to me in surprise. I shall look to Him with praise.

Prayer Reflection

Mine: It's funny, Father, how we sit around the boob tube and cheer ourselves hoarse over a football game 1,000 miles away, and utter nary a peep for a miracle of Yours right next door. I wonder whose side we're on?

—Questioning

Yours: _____

_____

_____

Give, and it will be given to you. A good measure, pressed down, shaken together and running over, will be poured into your lap. For with the measure you use, it will be measured to you.

Luke 6:38

46 GOD'S ARITHMETIC

She shared her problem with me as we sat on the lawn chairs in our backyard on a warm Saturday morning.

"Bob, I have only 47¢ in my purse. I have no money for groceries. I had to pay the electric bill or they would have shut it off. What can I do?" She spoke with deep emotion, in desperation, then added, "I didn't come here to beg."

I knew how difficult life was for this anxious one. She was lonely, fearful. She was both father and mother in the home. It was a heavy burden.

There was no question that I needed to help her. I didn't have to ask the Lord if I should—the question was how much to give. I thought of twenty dollars. It should buy groceries for the weekend. I told her that I would be happy to help. I went into the house to get the money.

At the desk I took a twenty-dollar bill from my wallet. The Lord seemed to say, "Bob, give her a hundred dollars."

I said in surprise, and, I guess, dismay, "Lord, I want to help, but a hundred dollars? I don't have that to give. You know we are putting money away for Rebecca to go to college."

God said, "Do you remember what happened just yesterday when you were balancing your checking account? What did you find?"

I remembered clearly. I had erred in subtraction in the running account kept in my checkbook. In the process of reconciling my checkbook with the bank statement, I discovered the error and found that I had one hundred dollars more in the bank than what I had originally thought. How I rejoiced when my mistake became apparent! It was like finding a hundred dollars.

And God wanted me to give away that hundred dollars?

There was hesitation on my part. But God was persistent. He made it clear. "Give her the twenty dollars in cash. It's Saturday and the banks are closed. That will meet her immediate needs. Then write her a check for eighty dollars. That will give her joy for next week."

Then it struck me hard—God's timetable. I accused Him with a smile. "You had this all worked out, didn't You?"

God smiled back, saying, "Sometimes I have to work things out for those of you who are a bit tightfisted with your money."

I knew God was right and marveled at His arithmetic. I gave my needy sister in the church the twenty dollars and the eighty-dollar check.

She said gratefully, "I'll pay you back when I can."

But I said, "No, the money was given to me for you."
Then I explained.

And we cried together.

Prayer Reflection

Mine: Lord, it's really not my money in the checking and savings accounts. You have supplied and blessed through education, work provided, skills developed. I would like You to authorize every check I write, sort of countersign it. Frankly, I don't trust myself. Be my Accountant.

—The Penny-Pincher

Yours: _____

_____

_____

Before they call I will answer; while they are still speaking I will
hear.

Isaiah 65:24

47 SPECIAL DELIVERY FROM GOD

Several years ago while serving as a Sunday school
superintendent, I was having no success at finding a teacher
for the youth class. Several qualified couples had been
contacted to teach the class as a team, but each had said, "No."

Finally the assistant superintendent and I decided that
one of us would have to take the class temporarily.

On the Wednesday before the new Sunday school year
was to begin, I was attending an evening prayer meeting at
our church. When sharing our prayer concerns, I mentioned
the fact that we had no teacher for the youth class.

A concerned group gathered around me, placed their

hands on my head and shoulders, and prayed for that specific need. I was glad for their interest, but still felt that I would be teaching the class myself on Sunday.

When I got home my daughter gave me two telephone messages which had come for me while I was gone, each asking me to return the call. I don't remember what the first call was about, but I will never forget the second one.

When I dialed the number my daughter gave me, I reached the home of one of the couples who had rejected the youth class assignment. The husband said simply, "My wife and I talked over that teaching position to which we earlier said, 'No.' There's really no good reason why we shouldn't take it. If it's still open, we'd like to take that youth class beginning on Sunday." I assured him the opening was still there, thanked him, and hung up.

I sat there shaking my head in amazement. Prayer I believe in, but this was too good to be true. What could God do for an encore? Wow! Talk about God being on time with His answers. This was fabulous.

When someone questions whether God answers prayer, I tell them about my experience. While we were praying, God was answering. It's too beautiful to keep to myself.

Prayer Reflection

Mine: It's almost scary, Lord, the way You worked that miracle of change in Harold and Christine Wenger's life and timed it perfectly in answer to our prayers. Thanks for doing the impossible.

—Bob Baker

Yours: _____

_____

Because of the Lord's great love we are not consumed, for his compassions never fail. They are new every morning; great is your faithfulness. I say to myself, "The Lord is my portion; therefore I will wait for him."

Lamentations 3:22-24

48 RJB TRANSLATION

I am probably the oldest teacher at our junior high school. Recently we went through a period of unrest and difficulty in our school. A number of the faculty were unhappy. The teachers' lounge abounded with gripes and groans. Teachers who rode to school together aired their complaints freely, looking for solutions, wondering if teaching really was worthwhile.

One morning several young teachers came through the school doors, their faces animated, frowning, their voices carrying down the hall to me where I was working on a display case.

I heard one of them say, "Let's ask Baker. He's been here a long time."

So I turned to where the teachers had stopped. Dick hollered down the hall to me, "Baker, what keeps you coming back to this school day after day, year after year? You don't even take your personal leave days. How come you keep teaching?"

Answers, reasons, flashed through my mind. I could say it was the money that brought me here, that I had no other profession; or I could say it was habit, something to do. Should I say that I was just hanging in there until retirement?

I walked down the hall to where the three stood with their briefcases in hand, faces already tired from thoughts of the day's activities and struggles, the defeats of yesterday dimming their eyes.

I said, "Fellows, to me every day is like a brand-new penny that is handed to me. It's another chance. Yesterday is gone, but today is here, a new opportunity. The penny comes fresh every morning. How I spend it is up to me."

My fellow teachers looked at me with some puzzlement. Dick repeated my words, sort of talking to himself in question form. "So every day is like a penny . . . a new penny . . . and it's yours to spend . . . or I suppose to keep, maybe throw away . . . ?"

They shrugged their shoulders, walked down the hall to the office to pick up morning announcements. I heard someone say, "Well, I guess that's one way to think about it."

I went back to the display case and asked, "Lord, did I say it right? Should I have said, 'This is the day the Lord has made; let us rejoice and be glad in it.' Maybe I should have said that instead of the 'new penny' bit?"

The eternal God smiled, patted me on the shoulder, and said, "Bob, it's not quite the way I would have said it, but for a beginner, it was all right."

God was right. At 60 I was still just a beginner.

I knew it was going to be a good day. It was like . . . well, it was like a new penny just handed me.

Prayer Reflection

Mine: Creator, when every day is the same, the challenges gone, and I face my work with dread, then give me the courage to leave, the grace to retire. When days are no longer new, it's time to go and be with You.

—Heaven-Bound R. J. Baker

Yours: _____

_____

_____

But when he, the Spirit of truth, comes, he will guide you into all truth. He will not speak on his own; he will speak only what he hears, and he will tell you what is yet to come.

John 16:13

49 HOLY SPIRIT MAGNETIZED

To clean our lawn spreader after using it, I remove the plate which regulates the quantity of fertilizer distributed. It's a simple process requiring only the removal of four special fasteners.

Last spring after fertilizing our lawn I removed the four wing nuts, laid them carefully on a newspaper beside me, and cleaned the spreader. In the process I also removed several handfuls of fertilizer and laid them on the same newspaper.

After oiling the spreader, I decided to throw the small quantity of fertilizer that I had removed on the daffodils.

Not until I started to reassemble the spreader did I remember the four wing nuts which also had been thrown on the daffodils. I searched for some time and found only two of them.

The next day, pondering how I might solve the problem, I thought of the powerful magnet in my classroom at school. I brought the magnet home that afternoon and swept through the rows of daffodils with it. I was immediately rewarded with two sharp clicks as the missing wing nuts were attracted to it.

As I rejoiced over the solution to my problem, I told God, "Lord, that magnet is just like Your Holy Spirit. He seeks and finds the lost sheep, the Christians who stray from Your fold, who get lost in the 'daffodils' of this world."

But God said, "Not quite, Bob, not quite. The metal of the magnet is really you. The magnetic force within the magnet, that is My Holy Spirit. The force can work only through you. If My Holy Spirit is to go sweeping through the 'daffodils' of this world, you must be the vehicle that carries Him to the scene of action. You are really the channel through which He operates."

I was impressed by what God had said. How easy it is for us as Christians to dump on God the task of searching for sheep who have strayed from the fold. God is willing to provide the power, but we become transmission lines through which that seeking, healing power flows.

Prayer Reflection

Mine: Being a Holy Spirit carrier is pretty heavy, Lord. Sharpen my sensitivity to his leading so I can keep your divine appointments.

—Often Tardy Baker

Yours: _____

_____

_____

I waited patiently for the Lord; he turned to me and heard my cry. He lifted me out of the slimy pit, out of the mud and mire; he set my feet on a rock and gave me a firm place to stand.

Psalm 40:1, 2

50 VALLEY OR MOUNTAINTOP CHOICES

Flying to a speaking appointment in the East, I looked down on the Pennsylvania mountains far below. It was a fall morning and one could see clearly how fog lay in the valleys, the mountaintops rising out of the white blankets drawn over every depression. I thought of the roads that wound through the valleys. The drivers must be having a difficult time. But when the roads spiraled upward and ran out of the valley onto the mountain slopes and tops, then the driver had a clear view and could drive safely.

I thought of our Christian journey, our spiritual pilgrimage. It seemed to me that God was offering us a bit more variety. True, sometimes there has been only one route, and it led through the valleys. There was no other way for us to reach the destination God had chosen for us except through the valley of trial, of sorrow. As with David, He was with us, even when we struggled through the shades of death.

But too often we take the lower route, travel through the fog-shrouded valleys instead of the alternative path that lies upon a higher plain. We travel the route of self-induced depression; we feel sorry for ourselves; we struggle through the clouds of jealousy and envy. We are encumbered by our pride. Our unwillingness to forgive another handicaps us and veils our pathway. God wants us to come up on the mountaintop, out of the foggy valley, to travel with Him in sunlit beauty, our spiritual vision unimpaired.

Job, Paul, even Jesus, had their moments of depression, their boils, imprisonments, Gethsemanes. But they did not stay depressed. They would recall that God was their salvation, that after death came the resurrection. Then they would spiral up out of their depression troughs, rising on the cresting waves of faith. And so, they lived 99.99 percent of their lives above the trembling elements, secure in God's hands.

Some Christians today seem to enjoy groping in the valleys, wandering on the slopes, consciously avoiding the mountaintop scenes.

Why? Perhaps they are afraid of the ecstasy that comes when they see God most clearly, when Jesus stands beside them, and the Holy Spirit ministers within them.

Prayer Reflection

Mine: Lord, when You choose the Valley route for me, let me go gladly, confidently, knowing You will walk beside me. But let me not take the valley route because I choose to wallow in the vale of self-pity when You are calling me to the mountaintops for rejoicing and fellowship with You.

—Wanting to Climb Higher

Yours: _____

_____

_____

So the wall was completed ... in fifty-two days. When all our enemies heard about this and all the surrounding nations saw it, our enemies lost their self-confidence, because they realized that this work had been done with the help of God.

Nehemiah 6:15, 16

51 THE BEST YOU CAN

When someone in my church is asked to fill a certain position and professes inadequacy to do the task assigned, I like to take them to the basement of our church to examine several rows of cement blocks on the north wall next to the furnace room. It is obvious that the blocks are poorly laid, probably by an amateur. Below and above them one can see the work of a skilled mason. It's obvious that the craftsman who worked above the imperfect area needed to make adjustments for several rows to compensate for the errors below.

I like to tell the reluctant church member the story behind

the crooked blocks, the imperfect wall. Years ago when we were enlarging our church, a number of us worked at the building after the regular construction crew went home. It was an arrangement we had with the contractor so the congregation could save on remodeling costs. One evening we needed some blocks laid, but none of us were trained in the mason's trade. Our "supervisor," Vernon Reiff, assigned me the job. I protested my inability, my lack of experience. He said, "Try, Bob, try. That's all we ask you to do."

So I tried. The poorly laid blocks were the result of those efforts.

The little sermon I preach in the church basement to the reluctant church worker is as follows: "True, the work we are asking you to do, may be imperfectly done. But it will be a part of the 'wall,' and that 'wall' will be higher because of your labors. Others will come along later, building upon your work. The Lord will enable them to correct errors you might make in attempting to serve Christ and His church. You can see that my work was imperfect, but it was the best I could do. It became a part of a solid wall, a part of this church. God asks no more of us than this, to do the best we can under the circumstances. To me, my wall is not a 'Wailing Wall.' It's a 'Praising Wall.' "

I don't convince every hesitant church servant to "lay blocks" for the Lord, but I convince some. And I reconvince myself.

Seeing those poorly placed blocks in that wall amidst the ones more correctly laid reminds me once more of my place in God's kingdom. As I look at my work of twenty years ago, a work still standing, a strange mixture of humility and pride flows through me. I am humbled as I focus in on my poor workmanship, thrilled as I step back and see the complete wall.

In spite of all my wretched efforts, I am still on the payroll of the Lord's construction company. Beautiful.

Prayer Reflection

Mine: Boss, some of my work for Your kingdom would have to be rated pretty lousy. But getting it done poorly was better than not getting it done at all. So thanks for using an amateur.

—Apprentice Baker

Yours: _____

_____

_____

They [Greeks] came to Philip ... with a request. "Sir," they said,
"we would like to see Jesus."

John 12:21

52 WASHING OFF THE CARBON

One day as I was typing with a typewriter that a number of
different people use, I was struck with the lack of sharpness
of many of the letters being typed. The "a" and the "e"
characters, frequently used letters, appeared almost as "o's"
with their central part completely filled in. They looked like
gigantic periods.

Lifting off the cover from the keys, I saw that each letter
was nearly filled with tiny bits of carbon and what appeared
to be threadlike debris from the worn ribbon.

I found a small brush and some alcohol. Carefully I
scrubbed and dried each key. My alcohol turned a bluish

purple and I knew I was helping to solve the problem. After the scrubbing and drying, I put in a fresh sheet of paper and typed briefly. Each letter was now sharp and clear, no solid "a's" or "e's."

As I sat there appreciating the improvement, I wondered about how clear a copy of my life was being printed. Paul spoke of his converts as being epistles (letters), "known and read of all men." I wondered if people were having any trouble reading my life, if parts of it might be a bit blurred, like the giant periods.

I sat there at the typewriter and prayed that God would continue His cleansing of my life, scrubbing it, washing it with the water of His Word so that as people read my life they might see the message of God's love being printed with accuracy and clarity.

Prayer Reflection

Mine: It's "sorry time" again, Lord. I know there are times when my Christlikeness gets covered up with Bob Bakerlikeness. Then people look at me and say, "If that's Christianity, I'm not buying it." Forgive me?

—Anxious to Be Clarified.

Yours: _____

_____

_____

Have mercy on me, O God, according to your unfailing love; according to your great compassion blot out my transgressions. Wash away all my iniquity and cleanse me from my sin.

Psalm 51:1, 2

53 THE HEALING

In June 1974 the principal showed me his anticipated schedule for the coming school year in our junior high school. I questioned a change that he was making in the science department I headed, expressing my concern. He explained his reason, but I still raised strong objections. I saw its short-range value, but I anticipated complications in the future. I let him know that I clearly disapproved of it.

When the fall schedule was finalized, I quickly noted that he had followed his original plans, ignoring my suggestion. As a principal that was his right.

But in my heart the matter rankled, the seed of resentment germinated, and I nourished it. During that fall I went about my school duties, but carefully and purposefully avoided any communication or contact with my principal if at all possible. I maintained a respectful but definitely a cool relationship with him. When he spoke, I spoke. Seldom did I initiate the conversation. I saved my smile, my approval, for others on the faculty. In his presence I was aloof, reserved, all business.

As the fall wore away, I thought I noticed some puzzlement on his part. Yet he was always polite, friendly, a gentleman. But I kept my distance, kept up the barriers. It was a part of my game plan.

As December advanced upon us, I felt completely out of tune with the Christmas season approaching. I knew the reason, realizing that I had acted like a child too long.

On the last day of school before our Christmas vacation was to begin, I stepped into his office and closed the door behind me. I described my attitude of the past four months, an attitude I could not justify as a Christian. I spoke of my bitterness which should not have been, and closed by saying, "I want to ask your forgiveness in this matter."

Gary, my principal, is a Christian, a considerably younger man than I. He rose from behind his desk, walked around it, shook my hand, and said quietly, "I appreciate your sharing, but you don't need to ask my forgiveness. Your bitterness didn't hurt me—it really hurt you."

How true. It was a memorable lesson the young principal taught the experienced teacher.

When I am disappointed, perhaps wronged, when I start to pout, I remember the conversation in the school office. Bitterness is not a cure—it's a cancer. As Christians we are never justified in harboring it. I am learning to live without it, and I am richer because of its absence.

We do not possess bitterness; it possesses us.

Prayer Reflection

Mine: Confession is not easy for me, Father. I so like to be right. Yet I need frequently to cleanse my soul in the sea of Your forgiveness. No alibis this time, Lord, just the humbling admission, "I was wrong."

—Spell Me s-m-a-l-l

Yours: _____

_____

_____

I am the vine; you are the branches. If a man remains in me and I in him, he will bear much fruit; apart from me you can do nothing.

John 15:5

54 MESSAGE FROM GABRIEL

When I was asked to substitute teach for one Sunday in the "grandpa" class at our church, I readily accepted. We never worried much about that class in our Sunday school. Almost anyone would do. One could always get a "good discussion" going to take up the time. Our concern in teacher placement was with the teenage class, the young-marrieds, the primary department.

I accepted, because I thought to myself, "Those fellows deserve a teacher who puts a lot of work into the lesson preparation, and I'm going to do that for the Sunday I teach. I'm going to throw everything I can into that lesson, really hand it out to them, treat them to something special, act as if they are the most important class in the Sunday school."

So I did. It was the lesson on the parable of the sower and the different soils upon which the seeds fell. I had illustrations, blackboard outline, questions, the works. I even passed various seeds down the rows for them to look at, emphasizing the science involved in that seed germination, its needs and steps in its growth.

When I sat down, I felt good. The men had been attentive, interested, involved. I had used audiovisuals effectively. I had not depended on a couple of controversial questions to occupy the time. I sensed that things had gone well.

Yes, I felt good. That is, until I talked with Gabe Yoder.

Gabe sat at the end of the rows. He accumulated the different seeds I had passed out, and after the class he returned them to me. They lay on his time-worn hands, a dozen seeds of several varieties and sizes. He thanked me for teaching the lesson and said, "I don't know much about seeds, like the scientific parts you were describing, but I'm curious about how seeds of different sizes can come off the same plant. I've noticed that they are not always alike."

Then Gabe pointed to two different-size seeds of the same variety—one plump, one wizened—and said, "I suppose seeds on the same plant could get different amounts of nourishment, couldn't they, depending on where they were located?"

I was gathering things up and said matter-of-factly, maybe a bit pompously, "Position on the stem or stalk might have some bearing on that. Keep it up, Gabe, and maybe you will become a biologist."

He gave me the seeds, shook his head, smiled, and said, "No, Bob, but I was just thinking. Maybe that's the way it is with us as Christians. Those that are closest to the stalk, the

vine, Jesus Christ, maybe they get the most nourishment
and become the plumpest Christians."

I looked up in surprise. That was a neat application. I told
him so. Gabe walked off, but his statement, his little alle-
gory, lingered.

But I also felt my spirits drop. And I knew why. My wonderful lesson kept shrinking—the preparation, the presenta-
tion. I was feeling like that wizened seed.

God came around that afternoon to talk about the lesson.
He knew how I felt and helped me to sort out the reasons.

"Bob, you did a good job on the lesson. Very scientific.
True, you never consulted Me about it, nor asked for Holy
Spirit leading. It was sort of a one-man show. But it was
good, polished. I'm not knocking it. But frankly, Gabe's
point after the lesson was the greatest observation of the
hour."

I said wretchedly, "That's it, I know. I know he didn't
mean to make it sound that way, but it felt like a rebuke."

The Father said gently, hand on my shoulder, "Bob, it
was a rebuke. I asked him to do it. I think you needed it. You
are younger than those in the "grandpa" class, but you are
not superior to them. You were not the plumpest seed there
this morning." Then God moved back a foot or so, giving
me a little space in which to think, to soak it up.

And I did. I thought I was the teacher. Instead I was
taught by both Gabe and God. Gabe had taught me more in
one minute than I had taught 15 men in forty-five.

I had already thanked Gabe. Now I thanked God and added softly, "Sorry, Lord."

He heard me, moved next to me, and put His arm around
me. And things got better, lots better.

Prayer Reflection

Mine: Father, teach me. When I think I know it all, rap my knuckles hard. I want to feel it. I know I'm asking for it, but that's because I'll deserve it.

—Show-off Baker

Yours: _____

_____

_____

The Lord is near to all who call on him, to all who call on him in truth.

Psalm 145:18

55 I'VE GOT HIS NUMBER, AND HE'S GOT MINE

We were on the same committee, and I was chairman. We usually met after our teaching day was over, gathering at one of the schools where we taught. But between our meetings it was often necessary to get in touch by phone. In the school personnel handbook I found all the telephone numbers listed for members of our committee except one—let's call him "Bill." Besides Bill's name was his address, but only a series of dashes for his phone number.

I called the operator, giving the name and address, requesting Bill's phone number. Quickly she informed me that his was an unlisted number and could not be given out.

At our next meeting I mentioned this to Bill and asked him for his telephone number. But he preferred not to give it to me. For some time he had maintained an unlisted number to avoid harassment. Recently he had even that unlisted number changed. The previous one had "leaked" from friends with whom he shared it to others and his trouble began all over again.

I was a bit chagrined, but he was adamant, firm. If I had to get in touch with him, it would need to wait until our next committee meeting. He did give me a number of a friend through whom he could be contacted, eventually returning my call. I thought to myself, "You trust him, but you don't trust me."

So went the year, with a bit of awkwardness between Bill and me. I wanted to understand, but Bill's distrust of my ability to be careful with his number bothered me.

Most of my problems with other people usually end up in God's hands for counsel, correction, clarification. One evening after being forced to go the long way around to contact Bill, while I was still seething, God got into the act.

He said, "Well, at least I don't have an unlisted number, do I, Bob?"

I liked that thought. "Right on!" Then I added, "And Lord, I never got a busy signal when I called You. Never a bill for long-distance calling. I never had to go through some angel secretary who said You would return my call at a more convenient time. I never got a recording that said your line was out of order. I really like Your service!"

Then I heard Him say, "Then next time you call Bill and start to clench your teeth and get all tensed up, think of that. I've got your number and you've got mine. We can talk anytime—no problem. Give it a try and see what it does to your bile output."

As Frances Hunter says, "God is fabulous!" He's so right on the advice. It worked. What was once a painful experience, is now pleasant. As I wait for Bill to return my call, I no longer grind inside, press my lips into that thin, hard line. I just keep saying things like, "Lord, You know that they say the speed of light is the ultimate speed, 186,000 miles per second. But they haven't considered prayer. Instant contact. Beautiful. No unlisted numbers! Halellujah!"

Prayer Reflections

Mine: God, I'm bubbling tonight. It's such a heavy thought. I keep wanting to say, 'Wow, wow, wow!' You're terrific. I don't know how You do it, but keep doing it! Keep my number posted right there beside Your phone. Thanks a million for listing Your ten-foot number for all the world to see.

—A Satisfied Subscriber

Yours: _____

_____

_____

Here I am! I stand at the door and knock. If anyone hears my voice and opens the door, I will go in and eat with him, and he with me.

Revelation 3:20

56 PULLING THE EARPLUGS

Some years ago as I studied a Sunday school lesson about Abraham, I found myself wishing that God would speak so clearly to us today. Frequently in Genesis the conversation is on a one-to-one basis, God actually talking out loud to Abraham. For example, in Genesis 17:1 it says, "The Lord appeared to him and said—"Although we know that God speaks to us through natural events, His Word, His ministers, and the like, yet we do not hear His audible voice as Abraham and other biblical characters did.

When such thoughts came to me, I would say, "Lord, if You'd speak that clearly, aloud to me so that I could be positive it was You, I'd go wherever you directed and do whatever You said."

But God said nothing back to me. Perhaps He wanted me to answer my own question.

In later Sunday school lessons I considered the simplicity of Abraham's life. And through that consideration I found a possible answer to my question.

Abraham was an uneducated shepherd, lived a simple life, slept in a tent, had no abiding city. He received no newspapers, listened to no radio, watched no television. He lived his life in slow motion and was not caught up in the rat race of the day. His mind was not cluttered by studies of psychology, group dynamics, or values clarification. God had a clean entrance into Abraham's mind and thinking.

I believe I know now at least part of the reason why God doesn't speak directly to us today. Why should He speak in such a manner? We are plugged into so many other sources of information that He has a hard time making a connection. When He calls He gets a busy signal. We are communication mad, so stuffed with input that it is coming out our ears.

God is still speaking to us, but the still small voice has little chance of being heard as we are living in the boiler factory of the world with the clanging demands it makes upon us. The soap operas of society have our attention.

Perhaps if we would draw apart, cast off the earplugs of the world, sever our roots instead of trying to find them, become mobile for Him, ready to move at His command, then we might hear God speak as clearly to us today as He did to Abraham then.

We say, "We're listening, Lord, keep talking." Then when He rings our number and finally gets through, we put Him on "hold." And there He stays until the connection is broken. Sorry, Lord.

Prayer Reflection

Mine: Lord, You are not in the wind, or the earthquake, or the fire. Your voice is lost in my activities, my words, my accomplishments. Help me to draw apart, rest, and listen for the still small voice. When you knock, I want to be home.

—The Busy One

Yours: _____

_____

_____

E PILOGUE

CHRISTIANS TALK TO GOD. Christians have long been interested in a kind of communication known as prayer. It is a type of communication in which we express aloud or silently our thoughts and desires to God. In our prayers we may praise God, ask Him for guidance, or make requests of Him. In the Bible Jesus Himself strongly suggests, in fact orders us, to bring to God our needs, to make petitions, to worship through prayer.

Most of us grew up praying. Quickly we learned to talk to God. When we became a member of His family, when we joined the church family, we were instructed on prayer. We graduated from asking the blessing, to leading the Sunday school class in prayer, to giving an invocation for the entire church. We became almost "professional." At least we become comfortable doing it. We believed in it and still do. Inspired by mottoes such as: "Prayer changes things," "Take it to the Lord in prayer," "More things are wrought by prayer than this world dreams of," "God answers prayer," we not only believe in it, we practice it. I say a hearty "Amen" to praying. I wouldn't be without it. I believe that I can talk to God at the drop of a hat. He's always on call. But does God talk with us? And how?

GETTING PERSONAL. A new Christian, after reading several articles of mine where I put God's words to me in quotes, asked with a bit of envy in his voice, "Bob, does God really talk to you?" I answered as follows:

God has never sent me a letter, regular or special delivery, a letter directly addressed to me, postmarked in heaven. Nor has He ever called me on the phone, collect or otherwise. I have not heard intelligible thunder from heaven. I have no scientific proof that He has ever so much as whispered to me. Yet, in another sense, He has used all of these media and more.

At the risk of being thought a bit strange, I need to go further. I believe God speaks to us through our wonderful minds. I believe He can manipulate the mind, cut in at His will over thought patterns of our own, direct our thinking, yea, even control it.

But how do I know it is God and not Bob Baker thinking? For me it is not hard:

> I am selfish, God is generous;
> I am vengeful, God is forgiving;
> I am sarcastic, God is gentle;
> I am impatient, God is longsuffering;
> I am forgetful, God is mindful;
> I am fearful, God is fearless;
> I am confused, God is clear;
> I am too busy, God is free of schedules;
> I am hateful, God is love;
> I am sinful, God is sinless.

Believe me, it's not too hard to sort out when God is calling and when Bob Baker is on the line.

There is a certain satisfaction, contentment, happiness, assurance, that comes from listening to God's voice. You know it's He. I guess you get used to hearing Him and recognize when He calls.

I believe God can play the tune, stimulate the neurons,

control the electrochemical balance involved.

If such a confession means that I am not playing with a full deck, somehow I'm not bothered. I like it when God is dealing, holding all the cards, handing them out at His discretion. Then I'm assured of always getting the cards He would have me receive.

You may ask, "Do you always hear Him? Do you always listen?"

To my shame, I say, "No."

Sometimes I'm too busy listening to Bob Baker. Sometimes I fold and toss in the cards He dealt me, afraid to wait and see what the next card will reveal.

I wish you wouldn't have asked those questions. But I have to be honest.

If by this time you are still wondering from where I'm coming, I must be very plain: I believe that God has facilities, the means at His disposal (both "up there" and within us) to plug us into His master switchboard. I believe God talks to us, and we can cultivate the listening skills so we can tune in and hear a live broadcast from Him. It doesn't have to be canned or on tape.

POSSIBILITY? The human brain weighs only about three pounds and uses no more energy than an ordinary light bulb. Yet, according to some authorities, this complex structure may screen 100,000,000 bits of sensory information per second, deciding what can enter and what needs to be blocked out so a person doesn't end up in a constant state of "seizure" because of the overload. But if the electronics industry wanted to duplicate the human mind by building a computer with similar capabilities, the completed project would cover the earth!

Will we someday find proof that God speaks consciously,

definitely, specifically to us through our minds, the uncharted "Antarctica" of today? Will new laws of thought communication be discovered? Will we learn to discipline and utilize our brains to transfer and receive thoughts, messages, and words, all coming through "clear as a bell"? I don't know.

But wouldn't it be interesting to have prayer, both sending and receiving, talking and listening to God, scientifically proven to be a possibility.

Until that happens, and even if it doesn't, I plan to keep on talking to God and listening to Him. What I am doing is not original with me. Thousands practice it daily.

Frank Laubach wrote, "Prayer at its highest is a two-way conversation."*

I believe it; I like it.

I think it's neat to be in communication with the Infinite.

Prayer, the Mightiest Force in the World (Old Tappan, N.J.: Fleming H. Revell).

Robert J. Baker, Elkhart, Indiana, has taught science in the public schools since 1947. *I'm Listening, Lord, Keep Talking* is his fourth book.

His previous books were *Second Chance* (a collection of short stories now out of print), *God Healed Me* (Herald Press, 1974), and *Insect Parables* (Herald Press, 1976).

His popular columns have appeared regularly in *Gospel Herald, Builder,* and *Christian Living* magazines. His resource for Sunday schools, "If I Were Teaching the Lesson," has been featured in *Builder* without interruption since 1963.

Baker received the BA degree from Goshen College, the MS degree from Indiana University, and the MAT degree from Michigan State University. He has also studied at Emory, Purdue, Ball State, and Indiana State Universities, as well as at Manchester College.

Robert and Anna Mae (Moyer) Baker are charter

members of Belmont Mennonite Church, Elkhart, Indiana. They are the parents of five grown children: Douglas, Richard, Nancy, Timothy, and Rebecca.

GAYLORD

PRINTED IN U.S.A.